POWER BASE:

Renewable

Energy

Policies for the

Nineties and

Beyond

WORLD
RESOURCES
INSTITUTE

Keith Lee Kozloff
Roger C. Dower

December 1993

Kathleen Courrier
Publications Director

Brooks Belford
Marketing Manager

Hyacinth Billings
Production Manager

Marcie Wolf-Hubbard
Cover Design

American Solar Energy Society; American Wind Energy Association; Atlantic
Richfield Co.; Earth Science Lab, Univ. of Utah Research Institute; Idaho Power
Company; Luz International Ltd.; National Renewable Energy Laboratory;
Northeast Solar Energy Association; SERI; Southern California Edison;
U.S. Windpower
Cover Photos

Each World Resources Institute Report represents a timely, scholarly treatment of
a subject of public concern. WRI takes responsibility for choosing the study topics
and guaranteeing its authors and researchers freedom of inquiry. It also solicits
and responds to the guidance of advisory panels and expert reviewers. Unless
otherwise stated, however, all the interpretation and findings set forth in WRI
publications are those of the authors.

CONTENTS

Two background papers for this report, "Renewable Energy: Barriers and Opportunities; Walls and Bridges" by David Moskovitz and "The Past and Future of Renewable Energy in California" by Gene Varanini can be obtained from World Resources Institute's Climate, Energy, and Pollution Program.

FOREWORD

Now that curbing greenhouse gas emissions has become a national and international priority, the United States needs an energy strategy worthy of the name. Using energy more efficiently is the place to start, but then we must go farther to stabilize atmospheric chemistry. We need a national strategy to encourage industries, utilities, and households to shift wherever possible from fossil fuels to cost-effective renewable energy sources.

A shift toward renewables promises substantial benefits beyond climate protection. Air pollution and acid rain would be reduced, making for healthier cities, crops, forests, rivers, and lakes. More use of renewables would be an economic boon too. Since solar, wind, and other such energy flows are inexhaustible, they can fuel economic growth in perpetuity. In the long run, they could supply all the power needed to generate electricity and to warm or cool buildings. Because some mix of renewable energy sources can be tapped locally throughout North America, renewables would reduce regional disparities in energy development and end the boom-and-bust cycles associated with fossil fuel production. Finally, relying more on renewables would shrink the trade deficits and security risks associated with imported oil and gas.

If renewables are so promising, why can't we just count on market forces to put them on the map? Keith Kozloff, senior associate in WRI's Climate, Energy, and Pollution Program, and Roger C. Dower, program director, answer that question in *A New Power Base: Renewable Energy Policies for the Nineties and Beyond*. Beginning with a brief tour through U.S. energy policies over the past twenty years, the authors demonstrate how policy zigzags have dampened renewables' prospects. They identify the key market, regulatory, and institutional barriers to greater reliance on renewables and outline strategies for vaulting these hurdles. They explore the major steps that government could take to lead the United States toward a renewable energy future, pointing out great opportunities at the state level, while stressing the important federal role in sponsoring renewable energy R&D and bolstering markets.

A New Power Base specifies what it will take to bridge the enormous gap between what renewables currently contribute to U.S. energy supplies—8 percent—and what they could contribute. The authors maintain that the first step is to reject the piecemeal policy-making approach of the past and establish a national renewable energy strategy that spells out complementary public and private roles in scaling the barriers to specific renewable technologies. Leaders from government and industry must collaborate in designing this strategy, they assert, because both are crucial players: the private sector must take the lead in developing and deploying renewables, but government policies must be revamped to ensure that renewables can compete fairly in the marketplace.

To buttress a national renewable energy strategy, the authors recommend that federal and state governments undertake three major policy transitions:

• Reform energy prices and tax policies that distort consumption or investment decisions, making these economic signals better reflect the full social costs of energy choices. Getting the signals right might mean enacting federal pollution or energy taxes, changing tax laws that are stacked against renewables, and eliminating subsidies biased toward fossil fuels. States could also use their regulatory clout to compel utilities to rethink public versus private costs. In picking new power sources, for instance, utilities should ask not only "What costs us least?" but also "What costs society least?"

• Encourage electric utilities and energy users to deploy renewables. With assistance from the federal government, state Public Utility Commissions should reform utilities' planning, acquisition, bidding, and contracting procedures to eliminate tilts toward conventional fuels. Utilities should also be encouraged to weigh renewables' often overlooked advantages—they can be installed in small chunks, for instance, and there's no risk of fuel price spikes.

As for builders and homeowners, governments or utilities could make renewables more appealing by spreading the word about their cost-effectiveness or offering financial incentives for adopting them.

• Promote private investment in commercializing renewable energy technologies. Some renewables will do fine once the playing field is levelled, but others will need investments in technical innovation or increased production capacity before they can become a commercial success. The federal government should develop specific commercialization plans for each immature renewable technology and invest public monies in ways that complement and stimulate private investments.

The analyses and policy recommendations put forth in *A New Power Base* extend and complement those contained in such WRI reports as *The Right Climate for Carbon Taxes: Creating Economic Incentives to Protect the Atmosphere, Solar Hydrogen: Moving Beyond Fossil Fuels,* and *Breathing Easier: Taking Action on Climate Change, Air Pollution, and Energy Insecurity.* To carry this work forward, the authors are now studying electricity generation in developing countries with an eye to identifying policies that can harness renewables to drive sustainable economic development.

We would like to thank The Energy Foundation and the Joyce Mertz-Gilmore Foundations, whose generous support made this report possible. We also wish to express our appreciation to those who have more generally supported the work of our Climate, Energy, and Pollution Program: The George Gund Foundation, The Joyce Foundation, the W. Alton Jones Foundation, The William Penn Foundation, the Public Welfare Foundation, Inc., and the Rockefeller Brothers Fund. For the foresight and sustenance tendered by all, we are deeply grateful.

Jonathan Lash
President
World Resources Institute

ACKNOWLEDGMENTS

We would like to thank all of the members of the Renewables Advisory Panel for their input throughout the development of this report. In addition, Charles Linderman, Jan Hamrin, Bill Keepin, and Helen English provided thoughtful comments on an earlier draft of this report. Many other individuals from the renewable energy industry, the electric utility industry, federal, state, and local government and other organizations generously gave us their time and their perspectives. We would also like to thank the authors of the four background papers commissioned for this project—David Moskovitz, Mark Trexler and David Burbach, Susan Williams and Scott Fenn, and Gene Varanini—from which this report greatly benefitted. From within WRI, we thank Walt Reid, Bob Repetto, Allen Hammond, Alan Brewster, and Jonathan Lash for their insightful comments. Of course, we alone bear responsibility for the accuracy and completeness of the information presented as well as the report's recommendations.

Special thanks go to Kathleen Courrier for skillful editing, Sue Terry for helping us obtain numerous documents, and Hyacinth Billings for managing the production. Last but not least, our gratitude to Eva Vasiliades, Cindy Barger, and Erin Seper for their continued support throughout the project.

K.L.K.
R.C.D.

RENEWABLE ENERGY PROJECT ADVISORY PANEL

James R. Birk, Electric Power Research Institute
Hap Boyd, U.S. Windpower
John Corsi, Solarex Corporation
John R. Dunlop, Consultant
Elizabeth Carol Ellis, Southern California Edison
Charles Gay, Consultant
David Holt, New England Electric System
Harold Hubbard, Hawaii Natural Energy Institute
Donald Klass, Institute of Gas Technology
Alden Meyer, Union of Concerned Scientists
Alan Miller, Center for Global Change
David Moskovitz, Consultant
Katie McCormack, Pacific Gas and Electric
Robert San Martin, U.S. Department of Energy
Scott Sklar, Solar Energy Industries Association
Randall Swisher, American Wind Energy Association
Marika Tatsutani, Natural Resources Defense Council
Emilio Varanini, Marron, Reid and Sheehy
Carol Werner, Environmental and Energy Study Institute
Katherine Zoi, U.S. Environmental Protection Agency

I.

CREATING A RENEWABLE ENERGY FUTURE—AN OVERVIEW

Encouraging the use and development of renewable energy technologies has been part of U.S. national energy policy for the last twenty years. Stated most recently in the National Energy Strategy, the objective of energy policy is to balance greater energy security, increased energy and economic efficiency, and enhanced environmental quality (U.S. DOE, 1991a). Following the energy price shocks of the 1970s, state and federal governments embraced renewables as a solution to national energy security concerns. By the early 1980s, however, this support had lapsed. Since then, renewables have regained government backing as an environmentally sustainable source of energy most recently in the 1992 Energy Policy Act. But twenty years of policy zig-zagging have left their mark. Renewables currently meet only 8 percent of our national energy needs and under current policy and market trends, this share is not projected to rise beyond 9 percent by 2010 (EIA, 1993). At this rate, the United States is unlikely to capture the full environmental and economic benefits of renewables.

In this report, current public policy for renewables is assessed, and state and federal policies for maximizing the environmental and economic benefits that the United States can obtain from renewable energy sources are recommended. Isolating the main market and institutional barriers to the greater use and development of renewables provides insights about where the United States has gone wrong (or right) in the past and how future policies may be more effectively targeted. The presumption here is that renewables are of practical, not just intrinsic, interest, and in general, the report emphasizes those policy options that allow renewables to fairly and fully compete in the market.

1

What Opportunities and Constraints do Renewables Face?

Renewable energy technologies make use of solar radiation, wind, running water, plant material, as well as geothermal heat. Drawing on energy from the sun, they are distinguished from fossil fuel and fission technologies, which are based on finite resource stocks. Collectively, "renewables" provide a diverse array of energy services. *(See Box I-1.)*

As discussed in Chapter II, the substantial environmental benefits of using renewables provide the most compelling reason for

---

Box I-1. Coming to Terms

Renewable refers to an energy source's potential to be managed so average annual energy output levels can be sustained indefinitely. A renewable *energy flow* (insolation, wind, biomass production, flowing water, geothermal or ocean thermal gradients, tides) can be measured only over time.[1] Except for geothermal heat and tidal power, all such flows are derived from sunshine. A renewable *energy technology* is the process whereby a renewable energy flow is converted into useful work of a specific thermodynamic quality. Harnessing wind and flowing water, for example, provides electricity or mechanical power, while insolation can be converted to, say, space heating or electricity. *(See Table I-1.)* In contrast, *energy stocks* refer to finite amounts of oil, coal, natural gas, and uranium at some single point in time, and a nonrenewable energy technology includes coal-fired steam boilers, natural gas furnaces, and nuclear reactors.

Several other key technologies do not produce energy directly but will be necessary to integrate renewable energy technologies into energy supply systems and match resource flows with local patterns of energy demand. Storage technologies (such as pumped hydropower, compressed air energy storage, batteries, superconducting magnetic energy storage, and sea-

---

taking a stronger public role in their development. Compared to other energy sources, renewables generate fewer air emissions and other environmental impacts throughout their life cycle. The benefits of ensuring that renewable technologies are available for widespread deployment become increasingly significant as the risks of global warming unfold. Carbon-dioxide emissions from fossil fuels (especially coal), which dwarf other human contributions to the increased risks of global warming, are projected to grow relative to other greenhouse gas emissions. Accelerating the contribution from renewables to the U.S. energy mix could substantially reduce

sonal thermal storage) enable variable energy flows, such as direct solar insolation and wind, to be used at a specific time and place for a specific purpose. (Other forms of solar energy, such as biomass and hydropower, are stored naturally.) High-power semiconductors allow electricity from solar and wind devices to be integrated into the grid without "power quality" problems. Increasing the distance over which electricity can be reliably and economically transmitted (with high power semiconductors, advanced control systems, and even superconductivity) helps match renewable energy flows with load centers such as large cities. Developments in energy-conversion technologies may also expand options for renewables. If biomass is gasified, it can be burned more efficiently than burning solid biomass. Modular fuel cells produce electricity with a hydrocarbon fuel through an electrochemical reaction more efficient than combustion and can use gasified biomass resources. In the long run, hydrogen (a versatile energy carrier) may be produced with renewable-produced electricity. Finally, energy efficiency technologies complement renewable applications in buildings by reducing energy requirements.

------

[1]While the energy output from individual geothermal wells has tended to decline over time, geothermal resources are included as a renewable energy source because heat energy is being constantly replaced.

Table I-1. Renewable Energy Technologies Classified by
Resource Flow and End Use

Resource Flows	Electricity
Solar Insolation	Photovoltaic Cells
	Thermal Concentrators for Small or Utility Scale Generation
	Solar Ponds
Biomass (Wood, MSW, Agricultural Waste)	Utility Scale Generation
	Gasification as Electric Generation Fuel
Wind	Small or Utility Scale Generation
Water	Small and Utility Scale Generation
Geothermal	Utility Scale Generation
Ocean Thermal	Small and Utility Scale Generation
Ocean Wave	Small and Utility Scale Generation

End Uses

Low and Medium Temperature Uses	Other End Uses
Flat Plate Collectors for Active Space Heating	Distillation
Sun-Tempered Design and Construction	Desalinisation Processes
Flat Plate Collectors for Domestic Water Heating	Detoxification Processes
Ground-Source Assisted Heat Pumps	Daylighting Techniques
Solar Cookers	Concentrating Collectors for Industrial Process Heat
Food and Crop Dryers	
Direct Combustion	
Gasification for Heating	
	Water Pumping
	Milling and other mechanical uses
Space Heating and Cooling; District Heating	

the economic costs of complying with international climate agreements. The country would also be spared some of the other environmental damages associated with the extraction, transport, and combustion of fossil fuels.

Compared to alternative means for reducing the environmental risks of energy production and consumption, renewables also have greater long-run potential to meet all U.S. needs for electricity and the energy used in buildings. As such, renewables could be a backstop technology for the United States that allows economic growth *and* complies with likely future environmental constraints. U.S. renewable energy resources total at least 200 quadrillion Btu's (or quads) per year. For perspective, total energy consumption in the United States in 1990 outside the transportation sector was 62 quads, and projections show that total growing to no more than 75 to 80 quads by 2010 (EIA, 1993.)[1] Resource constraints will thus pose no problem to increased reliance on renewables for the foreseeable future (though renewable energy flows do need to be matched to energy demands when and where they occur). *(See Table I-2.)* Moreover, compared to fossil fuels, renewable energy resources are widely dispersed across the country, so virtually every region can enjoy economic benefits from their production.

Renewables' large resource base won't be tapped, however, unless technologies are economically competitive. The cost of energy from renewables has been one of several factors constraining their growth. Fortunately, the cost of several renewable technologies is dropping. *(See Figure I-1.)* Even though the cost-effectiveness of any individual project depends on its location, design, and other factors, many renewable technologies are currently cost-competitive for diverse applications. *(See Table I-3.)*

In addition, near-term market opportunities for renewables appear large. Much of the nation's stock of electric generation facilities is due to be replaced: by 2000, the average age of power plants will be 43 years. Up to a fifth of the nation's nuclear plants may be closed over the next decade (Gilinsky and Bupp, 1992). Between 1993 and 2002, utilities plan to add some 82,000 megawatts (MW) of new, replacement generating capacity to meet U.S. electrical demand (NERC, 1993). Moreover, few absolute commitments to con-

Table I-2. U.S. Accessible Renewable Energy Resource Base and Contribution to 1990 Energy Requirements (Primary Fuels Equivalent)

Resource Flows	Accessible Resource[1] (Quads/Yr)	1990 Energy Contribution[2] (Quads)
Hydropower	5	3.0
Geothermal	18	0.2
Wood	10	2.6
Other Biomass (including municipal solid waste)	4	0.5
Ocean Thermal	0.1	0
Wind	57	<0.1
Insolation for Electricity	100	<0.1
Low Temperature Solar Thermal	9	0.5[3]
Solar Industrial Process Heat	5	<0.1
Total	**208**	**7**

Notes:

1. *See* Appendix B for assumptions, calculations, and references used to derive these estimates.
2. *Source:* Table A6, EIA, 1992. Estimates from Rader et al., 1990 are somewhat higher.
3. Does not include current energy contribution from passive solar gain.

struction of one type or another have been made relative to previous periods (Weissman, 1992). Within the last few years, several utilities have begun to help commercialize renewables (through partnerships with the renewables industry) and to acquire renewable generating capacity. Utilities in the Northwest, Middle West, and Northeast, for example, are laying plans for multi-megawatt wind projects over the next several years.

Figure I-1: Cost Ranges for Solar Technologies in 1980, 1990 and 2000

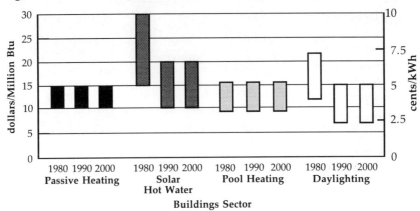

Buildings Sector

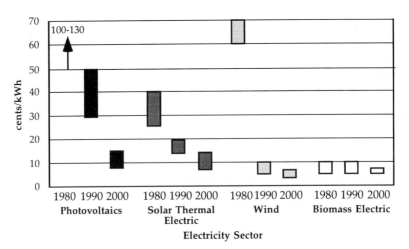

Electricity Sector

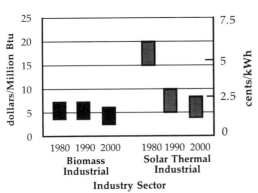

Industry Sector

Source: Larson, Vignola, and West, 1992.

Although greater reliance on renewables would serve the country's broad energy objectives well, the gap between renewables' actual and potential contributions is enormous. Except for hydropower, renewables currently contribute far less than the share that had been expected to result from early policy initiatives. *(See Box I-2.)* Part of this disparity reflects currently low prices for conventional energy, overly optimistic projections of cost decreases for renewables, and underestimates of the time required for any new technology to penetrate markets. Federal and state policies that affect how private energy supply decisions are made and, more specifically, those designed to promote renewables, are also at fault. Government policies have not effectively addressed the key market barriers that inhibit renewables' gains in market share.

These four primary barriers all divert investment away from renewables, thereby stalling development of so-called pre-competitive technologies or biasing current energy supply decisions toward fossil fuels.

• First, market energy prices do not fully capture the environmental and other social costs of various energy sources. Even though current environmental regulations force energy producers to internalize some of these costs, other hidden environmental costs, borne by the public, such as risk of climate change, make conventional energy sources seem cheaper than they really are. Price signals are also distorted by many government interventions in energy markets, such as tax subsidies for production and consumption, which favor nonrenewable sources of energy.

• Second, government regulation of U.S. utilities biases energy choices toward fossil fuel technologies even when renewables are more cost-effective. Partly because the utility sector evolved when energy options were dominated by fossil fuels, renewables receive short shrift in the resource planning and acquisition processes used by electric utilities. For example, utilities that use renewables aren't exposed to fuel price risk, and they can add renewable generating capacity in small increments, reducing the risk of installing too much or too little capacity. But regulation encourages utility decision-makers to discount these risks by allowing utilities to pass on associated costs to their customers.

Table I-3. Relative Competitiveness of Representative Renewable Energy Technologies for New Additions to Supply (levelized ¢/kWh in constant 1989$)[1]

Type of Renewable Energy Technology	Cost of Energy	Avoided Cost
Hydroelectric (new sites)	10–28[2]	4–7
Hydrothermal	7–12	4–7
Direct Biomass Combustion (baseload)	7–12	4–7
Biomass Gasifier w/ Engine (baseload)	6–8	4–7
MSW Combustion	0–12	4–7
Solar Salt Pond (NC)[3]	9(1996)	4–7
Ocean Thermal (NC)	9(1998)	4–7
Wind	4–5	5–10
Parabolic Trough/Gas Hybrid (Intermediate load)	9–12	5–12
Central Receiver (NC)	7–9(2002)	4–7
Central Parabolic Dish (NC)	5–10(1995)	7–12
Utility Scale Flat Plate Photovoltaic (NC)	16–22(current)	7–12
Ocean Wave (NC)	7–21(2000)	6–10
Residential Passive Solar Space Heating and Cooling	0–8 ($/mmBtu)	4–6 ($/mmBtu)
Commercial Daylighting	–3– –1	8–9
Residential Active Solar Water Heating	6–17	10
Active Solar Industrial Process Heating	2–5 ($/mmBtu)	4–6 ($/mmBtu)

Notes:

1. *Source:* California Energy Commission, 1992. Both the cost of energy and avoided costs are based on utility ownership and

will vary somewhat outside of California. While the avoided cost ranges reflect average fuel and capacity values, actual avoided costs vary according to regional differences in energy prices, energy facility ownership (investor-owned utility, government, independent power producer, or end user) and type of energy services being supplied. Avoided costs for baseload electricity technologies are based on a combined cycle gas-fired plant. For intermittent electricity technologies, assumptions were made about peak, mid-peak, and off-peak load profiles of specific technologies that make them more or less valuable to utilities because avoided costs vary over the three duty cycles. For thermal end use technologies, retail rates for natural gas or electricity are used for avoided costs (CEC,1992).

2. Upgrading existing hydro facilities is much less expensive than building dams at new sites.

3. NC means not commercial. Dates after cost of energy indicate projected cost for technology developed to that year.

• Third, the way that consumers and businesses make decisions about meeting their needs for energy services is often distorted not only by inappropriate price signals, but also by the high perceived investment risks, the high costs of acquiring information, or by the fact that much energy-using equipment is purchased by someone other than the user. As a result, a homeowner, for example, is unlikely to invest in a solar hot water heater, even though it may be very cost-effective when analyzed on a lifecycle basis.

• Finally, private sector investment in commercializing renewables is limited because no single utility or manufacturer can profit from all the future cost reductions that investing more in R&D might bring about. On top of this are the low returns and high perceived risks associated with any new technology and exacerbated by the government's historical intervention in energy markets. Everything being equal, sole reliance on the private sector for investment funds in research, development and demonstration projects means that the United States will underinvest in renewables.

11

Box I-2. Early Market Penetration Projections

There were at least eight efforts by 1981 to project the potential contribution of renewables to U.S. energy supply. Some studies sprang from detailed literature reviews and analysts' judgments, while others were econometric models of varying sophistication. The total renewable contribution projected by these studies for the year 2000 ranges widely, from 2 to 25 quads, reflecting analytical differences and varying assumptions about energy demand, technology, and price inputs (Holdren, 1980).

These early studies show how sensitive market penetration projections are, both to energy market conditions and policy, especially if extrapolated from an initially small supply base. For example, the actual increase in renewable energy's contribution between 1978 and 1990 was only 63 percent of that projected in the "business as usual" case of a study by the Mitre Corporation (which assumed that the federal renewable commercialization efforts in effect in 1978 would continue). Furthermore, the projected contribution from renewables doubles between 1990 and 2000 in the Mitre base case (Bennington, 1979; Holdren, 1980). In the business-as-usual projections from studies conducted just ten years later, renewables' contribution increases by only about 30 percent over the same period.

To be sure, many emerging technologies face similar constraints but the environmental characteristics of renewables suggest that without public support for investment, significant benefits may be lost.

Other market trends almost certainly affect the pace of renewable energy development too but do not, by themselves, justify government action. For example, most new generating plants added over the next five years will burn fossil fuels. While coal now commands about 56 percent of the electric generation market (up from 46 percent in 1970), the low prices and ready availability of natural gas will probably make it the dominant fuel choice for electric generation for the near term. *(See Box I-3.)* Although gas is relatively clean and abundant, and therefore an important fuel for electricity generation in the near term, its use doesn't mitigate global warming risks sufficiently, and supplies aren't ample enough to drive our economy indefinitely.

Also, some utilities are trying to wring extra years of production out of aging power plants. Given rising capital costs and mounting public opposition to new energy facilities, utilities have strong incentives to simply update or refurbish existing power plants rather than build new ones. While pollution-control requirements may rule out some attempts, if current trends continue, "life extensions" will increase to around a third of all generating capacity between 1990 and 2010. Renewables will thus be limited to competing for new plants, which will account for only a quarter of total generating capacity by 2010.[2]

At the moment, renewable technologies competing in energy markets other than that for electricity production (such as for space heating and cooling, water heating, and industrial processes) find low fossil fuel prices a barrier. Also, new investments in gas transmission and distribution pipelines made while gas markets expand represent a sunk cost that must be paid regardless of which other energy options develop. A further constraint on market penetration is the need to wait out the life of the current generation of energy-consuming equipment—ten to over fifty years, depending on the type of building, appliance, or industrial process.

Despite substantial opportunities, then, the combination of so-called market failures and other trends continue to inhibit the growth of renewables. In each of five recent studies, for example, the projected "business-as-usual" growth rates of renewable-generated electricity are quite similar, increasing modestly from about 3.5 quads in 1990 to about 6 quads in 2010.[3] And market forces over the next two decades may not change the picture much one way or another. According to one study, the difference between maximum and minimum contributions of renewable electricity in 2010 due to variation in oil prices and economic growth rates is only 4 percent; for nonelectric renewables, only 10 percent (EIA, 1993).[4]

In contrast to the modest "business as usual" growth rates, appropriately targeted public policies for renewables could cause fu-

Box I-3. Competition from Natural Gas?

How widely renewables are deployed to meet near-term needs for electricity and thermal energy depends partly on the price and availability of natural gas. The gas industry projects economically recoverable North American supplies to last 50 years at given current consumption rates and with today's technology. At current spot market prices, natural gas generation is attractive to electric utilities for new or repowered capacity because—compared to coal generation—it entails low emissions, low capital costs, a short lead time, versatility, and high-combustion efficiency. However, short-term gas prices have been volatile, and several factors, including the Clean Air Act Amendments and premature nuclear plant closings, could drive prices up over the next several years.

During the next decade, over 40 percent of all new electric generation capacity is projected to be served by gas. But, besides price, the extent to which utilities will turn to gas depends on supply infrastructure and market dynamics—the adequacy of pipeline capacity for future utility needs, the ability to match gas supply with generating plants' requirements, the size of investments in drilling programs, the availability of long-term contracts, and the effects of growth in utility demand on the cost and reliability of gas-fired electricity. Accordingly, the utility industry is exploring long-term approaches including the phased construction of combined cycle generators that can later be served by coal-gasification plants to reduce the supply and price risks associated with natural gas dependence (Moore, 1992).

One constraint to using natural gas to provide electricity and heat has been the limited network of transmission pipelines. Recent federal legislation to provide for equal treatment of Canadian and domestically-produced gas enhances the potential for gas to penetrate new regional markets, and the gas industry is planning major investments to expand its transmission pipeline network. Further deregulation of the industry may help hold gas prices down.

ture market penetration to better capture renewables' ultimate potential. In four of the market assessments just mentioned, at least one policy scenario is compared to a "business as usual" projection. *(See, for example, Figure I-2.)* In the comparison, market penetration of electric renewables ranges from 8 to 14 quads by 2010 under different policies that accelerate the commercialization of renewables or account for their social benefits. As Figure I-3 shows, these market penetration rates are two to three times higher than they would be under business-as-usual scenarios. Clearly, the future of renewable energy in the United States depends on the kind and level of policy support it receives.

What Does Past Policy Experience Teach?

Despite the importance of public policy strategies for moving the United States toward a renewably-based energy future, past policy initiatives provide only lukewarm encouragement. While the following chapters note some important success, they also make it clear past policies—poorly designed and implemented—did not achieve renewables' initially projected market-penetration rates.

Following the oil embargo of 1973, federal and state governments experimented with a wide range of renewable energy policy tools. As presented in Chapters IV–VI, these included investments in R&D and other commercialization activities; information programs; economic incentives directed at energy consumers or producers; utility regulatory reforms; reforms of codes and standards for buildings and equipment; and other initiatives adopted to facilitate the development and use of renewables. Federal research and development funding was increased rapidly on the basis of optimistic projections of technical potential and cost reductions. The federal Public Utility Regulatory Policy Act of 1978 enabled qualifying small renewable electricity developers to sell power to utilities.

Most states, particularly those that imported most of their fuel, also developed renewable energy programs. By the mid-1980s, for example, California had implemented a package of research, financial incentives, export promotion, regulatory reform, public information, and demonstrations that moved several renewable energy

Figure I-2: Renewable Electric Market Penetration

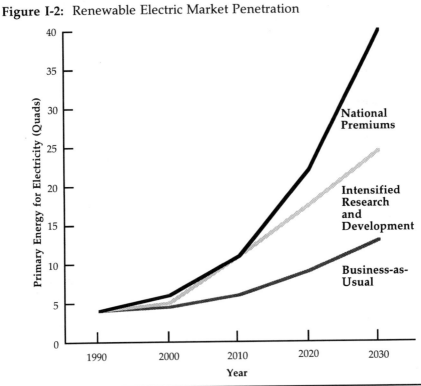

Source: SERI, 1990

technologies closer to commercialization and afforded the private sector experience in their development, manufacture, integration into existing energy systems, operation, and maintenance. States and the federal government alike adopted tax incentives to encourage demand for residential solar energy applications.

The federal government's interest in renewable energy, however, dwindled rapidly in the early 1980s as fossil fuel prices collapsed and as the Reagan administration's "free-market" philosophy took hold. While some state and local governments continued programs to promote renewable energy development, most were cut back or eliminated. With the reduction in tax incentives, publicly supported R&D, and funding for other commercialization programs, the 1980s

Figure I-3: Increase Over Business-as-Usual Renewable Electric Generation From Selected Policy Scenarios

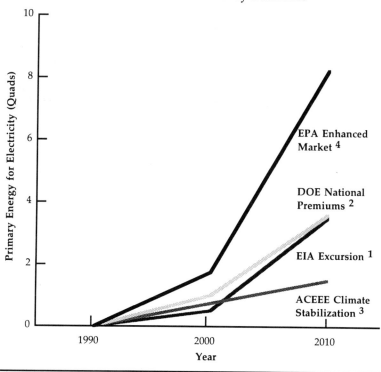

[1] *Source:* EIA, 1990.
[2] *Source:* U.S. DOE, 1990.
[3] *Source:* Alliance to Save Energy et al, 1991
[4] *Source:* Chupka and Howarth, 1992

found much of the fledgling renewable energy industry in direct competition with conventional fuels for the first time.

The experience of the 1970s and 1980s was neither an unqualified success nor an unmitigated failure. On one hand, policies toward renewables appear to have been more successful than for other new energy technologies (such as synfuels and the breeder reactor) that never yielded commercial energy. Indeed, modest markets for wind turbines and photovoltaics, two technologies

17

supported by policy, now exist. On the other hand, many of the renewables programs initiated in the 1970s were eliminated too soon and too abruptly in the 1980s to have achieved their full effects. Not surprisingly, investor confidence in renewables eroded during the mid-1980s and has yet to fully recover.

Partly as a result of this checkered history, the U.S. renewable energy industry saw only fitful growth throughout the 1970s and 1980s. As Figures I-4 to I-6 suggest, the level of activity in various segments of the industry in each year follows no consistent pattern. In the mid-1980s, for example, some segments of the industry (notably, active solar space-heating systems) virtually disappeared, while others became more concentrated as undercapitalized firms or those with less competitive designs went out of business.

Since the late 1980s, federal interest in renewable energy has again been growing, as evidenced by an increase in funding for R&D as well as other activities. The Clinton administration's first full budget contains substantial shifts in funding toward renewables. Just as important, the National Energy Policy Act of 1992 (NEP) contains a number of provisions supportive of renewables.

The likely net effect of this newfound interest as well as the impact of the NEP on renewables' competitiveness and future deployment is hard to gauge. NEP contains several provisions that promote the development of renewable energy—among them, investment and production credits, R&D support, and promotion of joint public/private ventures. But the Act also promotes nonrenewable energy through "clean coal" demonstrations, the streamlining of nuclear licensing, fossil and nuclear RD&D (research, development and demonstrators) and tax breaks for oil and gas production. And though the Act promotes independent electricity generation (by improving developers' access to transmission facilities and exempting a class of developers from the Public Utility Holding Company Act), independent power projects will probably continue to rely mainly on nonrenewable fuels. *(See Box I-4.)*

No strong evidence indicates that current initiatives and policies, including NEP, will avoid the pitfalls and limitations of past programs. Basically, public policies acknowledge the potential benefits of renewables, but have not prepared the way for renewables to compete for an expanded role in our national energy mix.

18

Figure I-4: Solar Thermal Collector Shipments and Trade, 1974-1984 and 1986-1991

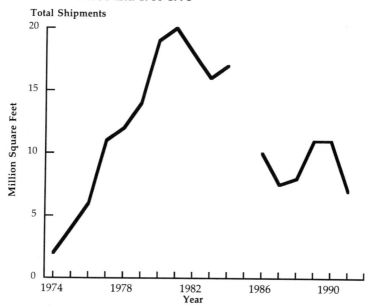

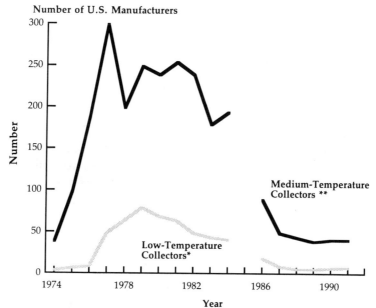

*Collectors that generally operate at temperatures below 110 degrees Fahrenheit.

**Collectors that generally operate in the temperature range of 140 degrees Fahrenheit to 180 degrees Fahrenheit but can also operate at temperatures as low as 110 degrees Fahrenheit.

Source: EIA, 1993b

Figure I-5: Photovoltaic Cell and Module shipments

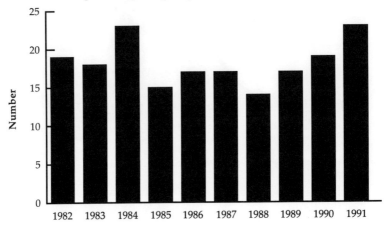

Number of Companies Reporting Shipments, 1982-1991

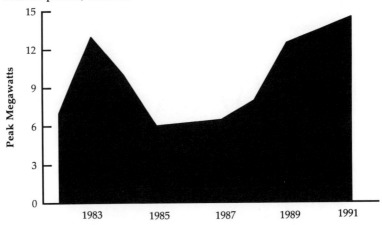

Total Shipments, 1992-1991

Note: Because vertical scales differ, graphs should not be compared.

Source: EIA, 1993b

Yet, from a systematic review of past and present public policies, several broad themes emerge, attention to which might improve renewables' prospects greatly.

Figure I-6: New Renewable Capacity (excluding hydropower)

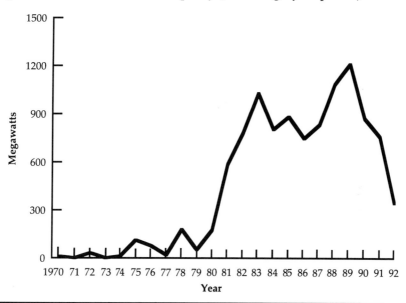

Sources: Data through 1989 are from Swezey and Porter, 1990. 1990-92 data
are based on several industry sources.

First, policy tools too seldom took the barriers confronting a
technology, or, more particularly, its stage of commercial development fully into account. Early federal commercialization efforts
stressed technological innovation, sometimes without getting feedback on cost competitiveness and the other features that make various energy services appealing to users. At the same time, subsidies to stimulate demand for renewables have been offered for
some technologies that aren't ready for commercial markets. For
example, early solar tax credits helped make eligible technologies
more competitive with other energy sources (Sawyer, 1986), but
did not give renewable equipment suppliers adequate incentives
to continue to reduce costs (Rich and Roessner, 1990).

The effectiveness of many past policy tools was also limited by
shortcomings in their implementation. Unpredictable and incon-

21

Box I-4. 1992 National Renewable Energy Legislation

The 1992 Energy Policy Act has several provisions favorable to renewable energy:

1. A permanent extension of the 10-percent solar and geothermal investment tax credits for business, currently subject to annual renewal.

2. A new 1.5-cent/kWh production tax credit for electricity generated from wind and dedicated biomass facilities built between 1994 and 1999.

3. A 1.5-cent/kWh direct payment to tax-exempt entities, such as public power systems, for renewable power production, though no funds have been appropriated yet.

4. A requirement that states consider adopting integrated resource plans for their utilities and promises of financial aid for implementation.

5. The inclusion of solar water heaters as eligible technologies under the Low-Income Weatherization Program, which grants money to individuals and agencies to weatherproof low-income housing. (Solar water heaters are also included in an Energy Efficient Mortgage Pilot Program, which allows borrowers to exceed normal FHA and VA loan limits by the amount of cost-effective energy improvements.)

6. The authorization of joint ventures between DOE and private companies to develop renewable energy technologies.

7. The authorization of DOE to buy down interest rates on private loans for renewable energy producers.

8. The establishment of guidelines for cost-sharing R&D programs.

9. The Act also contains provisions that, on balance, may work either in favor of or against increasing the relative contri-

sistent policy initiatives wasted public and private funds. For instance, extending energy-investment tax credits to business for only one year at a time—like a stay of execution—rendered them largely ineffective. Jacking up R&D budgets only to slash them bution of renewables: a. The partial deregulation of electric generation, creating a class of independent power generators exempt from PUHCA that can now build, own, and operate power plants and sell electricity to utilities. b. The authorization of FERC to require utilities to provide transmission access as long as pricing, reliability, and other criteria are met. (Currently, any electric utility, power marketing agency, or wholesale electricity generator can now apply to FERC for an order requiring another utility to provide wheeling services.) Qualifying facilities (QFs) under the Public Utilities Regulatory Policy Act do not have to give up their mandatory purchase status. These two provisions may help independently developed renewables compete with utility-owned power and use existing transmission lines to wheel electricity, but they will increase the competition that renewable QFs face from (nonrenewable) independent and utility-owned generation, both for supplying power to utilities and for access to transmission capacity.

The Act also contains provisions that adversely affect current and future hydroelectric development, and it authorizes funds for export promotion and technology transfer for several energy technologies, including renewables.

The 1992 housing bill also contains renewable energy provisions. A HUD-based Solar Assistance Financing Entity (SAFE), modeled on the old Solar Bank, would create a financing mechanism for retrofits and construction projects, including solar and other renewable energy building applications. If funding is appropriated, SAFE may give preference to programs that leverage funds from other sources. Recipients will mainly be people and businesses ineligible for renewable energy tax credits and the Low-Income Weatherization program.

within a few years dissipated accumulated expertise and made a smooth transition to privately funded R&D impossible.

A similar problem was that individual public policies, whether governing R&D or commercial deployment, were seldom coordinated to achieve maximum results and cost-effectiveness. No-where are these shortcomings demonstrated more clearly than in the experience of the solar thermal trough industry in the United States. *(See Box I-5.)*

Finally, estimates of cost-effectiveness were rarely used to decide the fate of a program or policy. Policy tools were evaluated infrequently and when they were, it was often on the basis of short-term measures, such as number of installations: no one bothered to find out whether sustainable markets had developed.

How Can the Benefits of Renewable Energy be Captured Better?

Analysis of the barriers that impede the diffusion of renewables and the lessons from past renewable policy efforts together form a strong starting point for ensuring that renewable energy technologies are available to the United States at a cost and quantity consistent with their economic and environmental benefits. While some of these policy shifts are new and reflect important though long-ignored barriers, others reflect adjustments to existing policies and tools. Some are already well-accepted; others reflect new perspectives.

A National Renewable Energy Strategy

The federal government should implement a national strategy to coordinate the selection, creation, and implementation of individual policy tools aimed at overcoming barriers to renewables' deployment. The strategy should recognize that the private sector must lead efforts to commercialize and deploy these technologies, but also that the federal government can level the playing field on which renewables compete with other energy sources for private investment. Accordingly, key stakeholders from both government agencies and the private sector must be involved in developing the strategy.

Besides the advantages of coordinating federal policy, a national strategy is important because some benefits of renewable energy (such as job creation) accrue to states, while others (such as mitigating fossil fuel emissions) go to regions or the nation. A national strategy could help allocate the costs and benefits of commercializing or deploying renewable energy technologies more fairly among stakeholders at various geographic scales. In addition, if markets for several technologies were aggregated regionally or nationally, costs would fall. The federal government is well-positioned to share and spread the risks and benefits associated with developing new technologies, and energy consumers across the nation stand to benefit from cost-reducing investments.

Visible and consistent national leadership could also guide the development of states' renewable energy policies. Without federal leadership, for example, state policies covering electric utility investments (power planning, site identification, and facility permitting), rate design, environmental compliance, and demand management are less likely to realize potential benefits for the United States as a whole. At the same time, a national strategy must recognize that many states are far ahead of the federal government in renewable energy policy, particularly in their regulation of energy supply decisions. Such state initiatives deserve federal support.

The new federal strategy should also recognize that renewable energy sources and the barriers they face are so diverse that simple one-shot policy prescriptions won't do the job at hand. On the contrary, while renewable resources as a group differ clearly from fossil fuels, not all renewable technologies and applications confer the same benefit equally. Each barrier to each technology needs to be addressed.

Three Public Policy Transitions

Three distinct shifts in public policy, described at length in this report, are needed within the context of a National Renewable Strategy to reduce the barriers to renewable energy diffusion.

1. First, energy prices and tax policies that distort energy consumption or investment decisions must be reformed. Market prices do not fully reflect the environmental costs associated with each energy alternative. Consequently, energy investment dollars flow into options with high social costs. As discussed in Chapter III, economic resources would be allocated better if private decisions more fully reflected the costs each energy choice entails. Correcting the prices of *all* energy technologies, is sound public policy for a host of compelling reasons.

Box I-5. The Luz Experience: A Case Study of Piecemeal Policy

Several shortcomings of past policy are exemplified by the experience of the solar-thermal electric industry. After dominating this industry for 11 years, investing over a billion dollars in its plants, and emerging as the sole supplier of parabolic troughs, Luz International, LTD declared bankruptcy in late 1991. At that time, Luz had nine privately financed plants in California's Mojave Desert producing 354 MW of electricity for sale to Southern California Edison. Although these plants still operate and parabolic troughs remain a promising technology for the U.S. (Mills and Keepin, 1993), plans for future plants have been shelved and the remaining assets sold to a Belgian company.

The Luz bankruptcy was brought on mainly by a loss of construction financing exacerbated by high interest rates for venture capital (*Sunworld*, March, 1992). Also, like many independent generators, Luz was highly leveraged, which contributed to its financial instability. But the failure of a major renewable-energy company raises broader questions about how effective individual policies can be in the absence of an overall commercialization strategy.

When Luz began operations, the local utility was offering very attractive buyback rates under state PURPA rules. Luz also enjoyed the fruits of federal solar-thermal research and a combination of federal and state tax incentives that sheltered the firm from market pressures. Indeed, federal and California tax credits together made renewable electric generation such an attractive tax shelter that investors were assured of a return on early projects through tax benefits alone. But depending on these tax benefits to obtain financing made Luz vulnerable since its electricity wasn't price-competitive without them. Delays in extending the California property tax exemption thus played havoc with project financing for later plants and, waiting out year-by-year extensions, Luz had to pay vendors premiums to meet tight construction schedules (Lotker, 1991). In the end, tax credits and property tax exemptions may have been counterproductive because they weren't stable and predictable.

Poorly designed tax incentives weren't Luz's only problem. Early contracts with the utility, which fixed payments for the first ten years of operation, were based on high projected energy prices. When energy prices fell in the mid-1980s by 78 percent, contracts with the utility for new projects exposed Luz's investors to price risk and the returns they required on investment jumped from 14 to 17 percent. But over the same period, tax support was halved (Lotker, 1991). With tax incentives and regulations that established contract terms insensitive to energy price swings, the technology was abruptly exposed to market forces.

Finally, public policies were not designed to fully exploit potential reductions in energy costs. The cost of electricity from the Luz plants dropped from \$0.24/kWh to an estimated \$0.08/kWh between 1984 and the construction of the most recent plant in 1990 (Gupta, 1991, p. 1995), and Luz officials had hoped to bring future costs down to \$0.05/kWh (*Energy Daily*, 12-3-91.) Had there been a full-blown commercialization strategy in force, government might have decided that it would be worth paying a premium for solar thermal electricity for a limited period if the technological advances made during that time would eventually drive down costs. But no such strategy existed, and since the bankruptcy the core of private-sector expertise in solar trough development has not been replaced, even though the federal government continues to support other pre-commercial solar-electric technologies. The Luz experience teaches that individual policies may not work if they aren't coordinated and implemented consistently.

Market-based approaches, such as pollution taxes, should be used to address this barrier whenever the environmental costs associated with different pollution sources can be estimated. Alternative mechanisms will need to be used when this is simply not practical. In any case, all pollution sources in all sectors and regions must be treated even-handedly.

Price signals affecting energy supply choices are also distorted by government subsidies that disproportionately favor fossil fuels and nuclear power. Distortions to energy investment decisions should be removed, such as from federal, state, and local tax codes.

2. Nonprice incentives that cause utilities and energy users to favor conventional energy sources must be reduced. In many cases, conventional planning and acquisition procedures work against renewable options, as does the way energy users make decisions. As discussed in Chapter IV, state PUCs should eliminate biases in utility-supply decisions by reforming utility planning, utility incentives, bidding procedures for acquiring new capacity, and contracting procedures. The federal government should help states undertake these reforms.

For end-use applications of renewables, current information programs, regulations, and incentives should be evaluated for cost-effectiveness and implemented as part of a broader marketing strategy for reducing building energy consumption. This strategy should take both non-financial and financial decision factors into account. As discussed in Chapter V, several policy tools now used mainly to promote investments in energy efficiency could be more effectively applied to renewables.

3. Government initiatives should promote private investment in commercializing renewable technologies. A commercially mature technology performs reliably; it is also cost competitive and supported by a marketing network sufficient to meet demand for products, maintenance, and parts. By these measures, renewable energy technologies are at various stages of commercial maturity. For some, policy reforms and initiatives that better account for the full value of renewables may be enough to meet a critical commercial threshold. But, for others, investments in technical innovation, increased production capability, or other preconditions to commercial success are needed first.

Policy tools, such as investments in technological development and demonstrations, public procurement, and incentives for private-sector investments and collaboration must all be evaluated as part of technology-specific commercialization plans. Each plan should identify how energy costs can be reduced, establish realistic cost-reduction objectives and timetables, and identify the public investments that can best complement and stimulate private investments. *(See Chapter VI.)*

Some Concluding Thoughts

Recommending cost-reducing and value-enhancing policy tools isn't enough to guide public policy toward renewables. In this era of fiscal austerity, the old axiom about "no free lunches" has to be taken seriously. Although the current administration has a more proactive philosophy toward guiding energy choices than its two predecessors did, the chronic budget crisis makes new initiatives that cost money a hard sell. Even if federal and state governments have the will, they have limited means.

Many of the policies discussed here, such as reforming utility planning requirements, involve only minor government spending. But other initiatives, such as public investments in R&D for specific technologies, can require significant expenditures. In any case, even though lack of data on the full range of economic benefits makes formal benefit/cost analyses of past renewable energy policies impossible, basic notions of cost effectiveness should still underpin future program decisions.

Throughout *A New Power Base*, the emphasis is on principles that promote cost effectiveness. Policy tools should be selected to match the barriers facing particular technologies, then designed and implemented to stimulate constant movement along the path toward commercial maturity. This means giving policy tools the time and resources needed to achieve desired results; making the period over which the policy is implemented predictable; and gearing the level of subsidies to buffer emerging technologies from extreme market swings without insulating the industry from all competition (thereby creating a "false market"). It also means tracking the performance of policy strategies so that future policymakers and program managers aren't in the dark.

The near and long-term benefits of renewables are substantial, but low conventional energy prices in the early 1990s make competition for investment at least as stiff as during the 1970s. Without a concerted push from national politicians and high-ranking officials—indeed, without a national strategy—payoffs from individual policies will be limited and renewable energy's enormous potential contribution to meeting national energy needs will never be fully realized. But the game isn't over. The United States can still put renewables to work and enjoy their economic and environmental benefits.

II.

RECOGNIZING RENEWABLE ENERGY'S BENEFITS

The gross disparity between the potential and current contributions of most renewable energy sources suggests foregone social benefits: environmental protection, economic sustainability, and, to a lesser extent, energy security and the widespread distribution of jobs and income. The loss of these collective benefits constitutes a major rationale for policies that go beyond current interventions in energy markets.

Environmental Protection

Since first receiving serious notice by policy-makers, renewable energy has often been touted as more environmentally benign than fossil fuels. As concern over global warming mounts, alternatives to fossil fuel combustion take on added luster. And optimism on this score is justified: though reliance on some renewables has land-use and other site-specific effects, long-term risks posed by renewables to human health and safety and to environmental quality do pale beside those of fossil fuels.

Mitigating Climate Change Risks

Virtually all renewable energy technologies emit only small amounts of carbon per unit of energy supplied throughout their fuel cycle.[5] As Table II-1 shows, a gas-fired power plant—the "cleanest" of the fossil-fuel technologies—still emits many times more carbon than all other renewable technologies except ocean thermal. What's more, carbon emissions during operation dwarf those that occur during fuel extraction and operation for virtually all other sources. In sharp contrast, most renewables contribute to carbon emissions

Table II-1. CO_2 Emissions From Electric Generation

Technologies	Metric Tons per GWh
Conventional Coal Plant	964.0
Atmospheric Fluidized Bed Combustion Coal	962.9
Plant Integrated Gasification Combined Cycle	
Electric Plant	750.9
Oil-Fired Plant	762.2
Gas-Fired Plant	484.0
Ocean Thermal Energy Conversion	304.0
Geothermal Steam	56.8
Small Hydropower*	10.0
Boiling-Water Reactor	7.8
Wind Energy	7.4
Photovoltaics	5.4
Solar Thermal	3.6
Large Hydropower*	3.1
Wood (sustainable harvest)	-159.9

* This analysis considered only construction of new dams.
Source: San Martin, 1989.

only during their manufacture.[6] Biomass, open-cycle geothermal steam, and ocean thermal are exceptions since they release carbon dioxide during energy extraction (McGowan, 1991).

While carbon emissions from renewable energy sources are tiny compared to those from fossil fuels, they do vary—depending on which renewable energy flows are captured, how they are managed, and which "end use" energy services are supplied. For example, biomass can be burned directly for space heating, used to generate electricity, or converted to a gaseous or liquid fuel; how much carbon it gives off during its lifecycle depends on how it is grown, whether fossil fuels are used in feedstock production, and how efficiently it is harvested, transported, and burned. Indeed, biomass fuel cycles can entail either negative or positive net emissions (Trexler, 1991).

One way to assess the environmental benefits of reducing carbon emissions by relying more on renewable energy is to add up the costs of current energy use. One preliminary effort to assign a dollar value to the loss in agricultural production and to other environmental damages associated with long-term climate change from a doubling of atmospheric CO_2 concentrations pegs damages at roughly 0.5 percent of GNP for the United States (Nordhaus, 1991). But such estimates should be considered largely speculative and—since many categories of potential environmental loss that could far outweigh more direct economic losses have yet to be quantified—highly conservative.

Another more recent analysis of the economic damages to the United States from climate change gives more inclusive estimates in the range of 1 to 2 percent of U.S. gross domestic product (GDP)[7]—or around $60–$117 billion annually (Cline, 1992a). This estimate excludes any economic losses associated with atmospheric CO_2 concentrations that go beyond a twofold increase, even though the doubling point would almost certainly be passed by 2050 or so if no efforts were made to reduce CO_2 emissions. Damages from a 10°C global warming, which could occur by the 22nd century, are estimated at 6 percent of U.S. GDP.

Several studies, (among them, Chupka and Howarth, 1992; Lashof and Tirpak, 1990) have concluded that deploying more renewables could substantially reduce carbon emissions, and, consequently, any "commitment" to global warming. One approach to measuring the economic value of these carbon reductions is to compare the costs to the economy of curbing carbon emissions with and without relying more on renewables. In the Global 2100 model developed by Manne and Richels, gross GDP and consumption losses associated with reducing carbon emissions can be estimated, though the social benefits of curbing emissions or recycling carbon tax revenues are not taken into account (Manne and Richels, 1992).[8]

WRI ran this model for two renewable electricity generation cases approximating scenarios in the 1990 DOE White Paper on renewables (SERI, 1990): Business as Usual (assuming that there will be no public policies to promote the deployment of renewables) and National Premiums (assuming that an energy-market price premium of 2 cents/kWh is applied to enhance the competitiveness of electric renewables and that market penetration is not constrained by the intermittency of solar and wind resources). Under the second scenario, renewable electric generation supplies about 37 quads by 2030—more than three times that under the Business as Usual scenario. In both scenarios run by WRI, the assumption is that U.S. emissions would be held at 1990 levels until 2000 and then reduced by 20 percent by 2010.

The simulated economic benefits of developing renewable electric options are substantial. Over the period analyzed, annual GDP losses under the renewable-intensive scenario are as much as one third lower than those incurred otherwise. As Figure II-1 shows, GDP losses are cut from, for example, about 3 percent to 2 percent in 2040. The present value of cumulative consumption losses is also $1.7 trillion (discounted at a social rate of 3 percent) less in the National Premiums case. If the non-electric application of renewables were considered, GDP losses would presumably fall even more.

Aside from their macroeconomic effects, how do renewables compare in total carbon-reduction potential and cost effectiveness with other actions aimed at reducing carbon? As Table II-2 shows, renewables display a wide range of cost-effectiveness, and several compare favorably with other electric supply technologies.

Nuclear fission, another supply-side option for reducing carbon emissions, has several disadvantages compared to renewables. As a group, renewables can supply a more diverse range of energy services than fission technologies, which provide only base-load electricity. Compared to acceptable nuclear options, the cost of further developing precommercial renewable technologies (in the event that fossil fuels must be widely replaced) appears low. And the cost effectiveness of reducing carbon emissions by shifting to fission is highly sensitive to such unknown "downstream" costs as those of nuclear waste disposal and plant decommissioning.[9]

While valuable for several reasons, energy efficiency improvements alone can't bring overall carbon dioxide emissions down and hold them there (Schipper, 1991; Green, 1992). Several studies conclude that a combination of energy-efficiency technologies can reduce some carbon emissions at net negative cost (Jackson, 1991; Kreith et al., 1991; Krause et al. 1992). Such estimates, of course, de-

Figure II-1: Global Warming Benefits from Renewable
Electric Generation

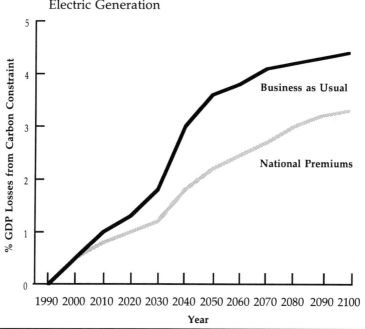

Source: World Resources Institute

pend on assumptions about the costs and carbon emissions associated with manufacturing, marketing, and installing efficiency improvements. Furthermore, while cost-saving or low-cost efficiency improvements can provide initial one-time savings in carbon emissions, greater investments will eventually be required to offset emission growth trends over time (Cline, 1992b). Carbon reduction from energy-efficiency improvements will be limited by market saturation and, eventually, by thermodynamic limits. Also, efficiency improvements stimulate economic growth, which entails energy consumption (Saunders, 1992).

Other Environmental Benefits

Apart from climate, many other environmental resources are affected by energy production. Among others, these include air

Table II-2. Relative Cost Effectiveness of CO_2 Reduction from Selected Electric Technologies

Technology	Reduction in Metric Tons/GWh Relative to Conventional Coal Plant[1]	Incremental $/Metric Ton Reduction[2]
IGCC Electric Plant	213	$47–$141
Gas-fired Plant	480	$0
Geothermal	907	$0
Boiling-Water Reactor	956	$21–$31
Wind	956	$10
Photovoltaic	959	$62–$73
Solar Thermal	960	$10–$20
Large Hydropower	961	$10–$31
Biomass Direct Combustion	1,124	$0–$9

Notes:
1. From Table III-1.
2. Calculation based on Table II-3.

quality, water quantity and quality, land resources, material resources, ecosystems, human health and safety, and aesthetic, cultural, and recreational values. Some of these potential impacts are highly site-specific, but others are not.

Table II-3 compares the materials requirements, land-use effects, pollution associated with energy extraction, facility construction, and the operation of three energy technologies. As the Table shows, central-station photovoltaics have the lowest emissions or material requirements in four categories and the highest in only one. (PV modules incorporated into existing structures would be even less materials-intensive than free-standing applications.)

Like certain other impacts unrelated to site, emissions of heavy metals and radioactivity are not factored into this comparison. Arsenic, selenium, cadmium, mercury, and the other elements in coal pose environmental risks because they are toxic and they accumulate in biological systems. Some such metals are also used in the manufacture of certain types of photovoltaic cells, but they are locked in materials that can more readily be kept from entering ecological systems.

As for other air pollutants associated with fossil fuels, greater use of renewable energy technologies could significantly reduce most.[10] According to an analysis of how enhanced penetration of renewables would affect different regions, additional windpower would prevent the most NO_x and particulates *(See Table II-4.)* Since biomass will be burned mostly in regions where high-sulfur coal would otherwise be used, it is estimated to be more effective than solar thermal and geothermal technologies at reducing SO_2. In all,

Table II-3. Energy System Emissions and Material Requirements

	AFBC Plant	Boiling Water Reactor	PV Central Station
CO_2 Emissions (Tons/GWh)	1057.09	5.59	5.89
NO_x Emissions (Tons/GWh)	1.55	0.034	0.008
SO_x Emissions (Tons/GWh)	2.97	0.030	0.02
Particulate Emissions (Tons/GWh)	1.62	0.00	0.02
Coal Waste (Tons/GWh)	142.69	NA	NA
Land Utilization (Acres/GWh)	0.09	0.03	0.08
Steel Utilization (Tons/GWh)	0.22	0.20	1.84

Source: San Martin, 1989.

SO_2 reductions from enhanced renewables deployment could conceivably drive aggregate national emissions below the cap mandated by the Clean Air Act Amendments. The "enhanced market penetration" scenario would reduce national SO_2 emissions from all sources by 14 percent and NO_x emissions by 9 percent, compared to 3 percent and 2 percent, respectively, in a business-as-usual case (Chupka and Howarth, 1992).

Yet, not all renewable energy projects entail clear environmental benefits. For instance, a 100-MW wind farm with a low capacity factor may not offset as much sulfur dioxide from existing coal-fired capacity as a 100-MW combined cycle gas plant with a high capacity factor does (Sim and Waters, 1992). And whether environ-

Table II-4. National Air Pollution Prevented from Renewables Enhanced Market Scenario

Technology	Incremental Generation 1990–2010 (GWh Yr)	Air Pollution Prevented 1990–2010 (Thousand Metric Tons/Yr)			
		SO_2	NO_X	Particulate Matter	CO
Biomass Electric Solid	344,464	2,515.4	818.2	-28.9	-480.26
Biomass Electric MSW	37,071	220.4	48.7	-381.98	-15.15
Biomass Electric Gas	11,547	52.4	-50.0	1.87	-33.12
Geothermal Electric	133,935	225.2	389.6	13.52	21.36
Hydropower	45,508	271.7	176.6	10.32	6.70
Photovoltaic	195,040	891.7	689.5	37.06	29.64
Solar Thermal	114,323	142.4	361.3	13.00	18.14
Windpower	139,675	602.9	567.2	33.68	20.46
Total	1,021,563	4,922.1	3,001.3	-301.42	-432.23

Source: Chupka and Howarth, 1992.

mental quality improves with greater use of municipal solid waste combustion depends on whether effective emission-control technologies are used and on whether landfilling or recycling is the waste-disposal method displaced.

By definition, site-related impacts vary by location. But estimates of energy technologies' relative land intensity provide the basis for a first-order comparison of such impacts. Although some renewable technologies require much more land than others, renewables as a class don't necessarily require more land than fossil fuel technologies do if the whole fuel cycle is taken into account. *(See Table II-5.)* Indeed, PV central station technologies are relatively land-intensive, but PV building applications are not. Furthermore, "big hydro" facilities are used for irrigation and flood control, as well as for power generation. PV, wind, and solar-thermal equipment can be removed, so the land can be restored. Biomass plantations are by far the most land-intensive renewable technology, but growing crops for energy rather than food may not require a major land use change.

Some of the impacts associated with certain renewables do require special attention. Conventional hydropower facilities have well-known effects on river ecosystems. Wind facilities are hard to hide because wind resources tend to be greater along ridges, passes, and other high-elevation locations and because more energy can be captured by larger wind machines, which protrude further above the horizon. (On the other hand, wind electricity production is compatible with other land uses, such as grazing.) Geothermal steam sites are often in or next to protected areas prized for their unusual geological characteristics. Biomass energy projects, depending on feedstock management practices, can reduce or enhance ecosystem diversity. But while all energy production technologies have site-related impacts, no renewables except perhaps biomass entail fuel-extraction, processing, and transport impacts anything like those associated with fossil fuels.

Economic Sustainability

All renewable energy flows provide useful energy services for the indefinite future. Theoretically then, with renewable technolo-

Table II-5. Fuel Cycle Land Requirements for Electric Generation Technologies

Technology	M^2/GWh
Gas Turbine	25–80
Lignite Coal	800
Bituminous Coal	80–400
Integrated Gasification Combined Cycle	300
Nuclear	80–100[1]
PV Central Station	300–700
Wind	40–1,700
Large Hydro	1,000–30,000
Small Hydro	20–2,000
Solar Thermal Trough	100–400
Dedicated Biomass Plantation	15,000–30,000

Sources: Anderson, 1992; Smil, 1991; Winter, 1991; Elliot, et al., 1990; Winter et al., 1990; Meridian, 1989.
1. Does not include back end of the nuclear fuel cycle.

gies, the U.S. economy could substitute abundant production inputs for increasingly scarce fossil-fuel inputs. The development of a commercially viable backstop for fossil fuels would also help hold energy prices down, much as the discovery of a major new fossil fuel resource does (Dasgupta and Heal, 1981). Indeed, if energy markets functioned as economic textbooks say they should, energy price trends would signal the need to develop such a backstop technology and fossil fuels would be then displaced as their prices rose to the cost of the backstop (Nordhaus, 1973; Tietenberg, 1988). But such a smooth transition could occur only if markets performed on the basis of perfect foresight about resource scarcity. Moreover, long-term scarcity trends may be obscured by short-term political interventions, actions by major energy importers or exporters to control demand or supply, and fluctuations in demand.

In the real world, economic and physical indicators of global fossil-fuel scarcity as a group suggest that there is currently little impetus to accelerate the development of backstop technologies. *(See Box II-1.)* Alone, the present value of the benefits of developing renewable technologies to replace fossil fuels in the distant future doesn't justify the effort. Because coal reserves are relatively well-documented, because they are expected to far outlast other fossil fuel resources, and because coal can be transformed into liquid and gaseous fuels, fossil-fuel scarcity is ultimately a function of coal scarcity, and coal is plentiful. Moreover, even though the market uses a higher discount rate than the optimal social discount rate (Lind et al., 1982), events occurring in 200 years (such as fossil fuel restrictions) carry little economic weight now. For this reason, the inability of energy markets to fully incorporate future generations' energy service preferences increases the gap between the private and social value of renewable energy very little.

Sustainability Benefits Not Reflected in Energy Markets

Even if fossil fuel scarcity per se does not justify accelerating the development of renewables, a social objective of making energy supplies sustainable might. If the goal were to make sure that current resource consumption does not reduce future environmental and economic wealth, there would be two reasons to slow the depletion of current energy stocks. First, as the largest fossil-fuel contributor to greenhouse gas emissions per unit of energy content, coal combustion is likely to be increasingly restricted either unilaterally or multilaterally. Restricting coal use to reduce climatic or other environmental risks would greatly boost demand for oil and natural gas, perhaps to levels that couldn't be met by these fuels.

Second, fossil fuel use might be constrained to secure future generations' access to energy services at fair prices. Even though supplying energy services from energy income (renewable energy flows) may be more expensive than drawing down energy capital (fossil and nuclear fuel stocks), only the first tack keeps energy services available indefinitely. To guarantee a constant flow of energy services, our generation would need to invest in energy-producing equipment and technology that produce at least as much energy service as our generation consumed. It would, in other words, have to begin setting aside funds now for developing renewable energy technologies. The necessary reinvestment surcharge—a function of

41

Box II-1. Fossil Fuel Scarcity

Fossil fuel scarcity is a function of energy demand, physical stocks, and the technologies available to find and extract those stocks and convert them into useful work. Different economic and physical measures give varying impressions of the extent of fossil-fuel scarcity in the United States and the world. Because all measures have shortcomings (Tietenberg, 1988), a full picture of resource scarcity can be gleaned only by examining several measures.[1]

One commonly used economic measure is energy price. Even though market prices differ from those that would prevail in perfectly operating markets, long-term price trends are still useful. According to federal government projections, the annual constant dollar increase in price between 1990 and 2010 is projected to be 1.3 percent for oil, 3.7 percent for gas, and 1.6 percent for coal (EIA, 1993).

Physical measures of scarcity indicate that the global fossil-fuel resource base is large enough to support economic activities for hundreds of years (although fossil energy will become more expensive as lower quality reserves are extracted). For the world, 14 percent of total gas resources and 29 percent of oil (including cumulative production, identified reserves, and undiscovered resources), respectively, are estimated to have been consumed by 1988. One study estimates that these resources will be all but depleted before the middle of the next century (Masters et al., 1990). But another measure, the reserve-to-production ratio,[2] has not been indicating consistent increases in

technology-development costs, depletion rates of fossil-fuel stocks, and population and energy consumption trends—would increase as fossil-fuel stocks were drawn down and would, according to one estimate, reach $0.80/kWh by 2050 (Hohmeyer, 1992a). While the size of the required surcharge is clearly debatable, the "sustainability value" of renewables might be much greater than that suggested by fossil fuel scarcity alone.

scarcity. As of 1989, the reserve-to-production ratio for the world stood at 43 years for crude oil, 61 years for natural gas, and over 200 years for coal (Masters et al., 1991). In fact, improvements in exploration, extraction, processing, and energy-generation technologies have mitigated downward pressure on reserve-to-production ratios. (The potential for further productivity gains is unknown.)

In general, fossil fuels are becoming scarcer in the United States than in the world as a whole. In the United States, cost reductions from technical change overshadowed the cost increases stemming from oil depletion between 1936 and the mid-1960s. Thereafter, however, the cost increases overwhelmed cost reductions, and today few policies for enhancing domestic supply seem feasible (Kaufmann and Cleveland, 1991). Another measure of supply, the energy return on investment in resource extraction, also indicates that coal and oil are growing scarcer in the United States (Hall and Cleveland, 1981; Cleveland, 1992).

---

[1]For example, economic indicators of fossil fuel scarcity are based on theoretical models that reflect unrealistic assumptions that resource allocators are aware of the total stock of resources, the course of technological development, and the level of demand throughout the future. Moreover, empirical estimates of resource scarcity based on energy prices could reflect either actual fossil fuel scarcity or the assumption that resource allocators are informed about the total stock of resources (Norgaard, 1990; Norgaard, 1991).

[2]The ratio of known reserves in a given year to production in that year gives the number of years current levels of consumption can be sustained.

Potential environmental constraints on coal combustion and intergenerational equity considerations argue for accelerating renewable technologies' entrance into the energy markets now served by fossil fuels. Conventional natural gas stocks are currently projected to last until around 2050. But, as discussed in Chapter I, market forces alone are unlikely to allow renewables to saturate the market by then. And if these technologies follow the Sshaped curve of market penetration that several other energy sources have, market share will not reach 50 percent until a century after they are introduced (Marchetti and Nakicenovic, 1979). Moreover, the average time required for several electric technologies (nuclear, diesels, pulverized coal, and heat pumps) to move from scientific demonstration to market penetration of 10 percent or more has been about 57 years. (Nuclear fission took the least time because it received substantial public support.)

Increased Energy Security

The United States has grown increasingly dependent on petroleum imports since the oil crises of the 1970s. Today, over 70 percent of the world's recoverable oil and gas lie in five basins, all outside the United States (Smil, 1991). By 2010, net oil imports are projected to comprise 52 to 72 percent of total oil consumption, compared to 42 percent in 1990. Net gas imports are projected to reach 17 percent of total consumption by 2010 (Energy Information Administration, 1993).

Petroleum dependence makes the U.S. economy vulnerable to oil-market disruptions caused by political upheavals, military actions, or sudden or dramatic price increases by oil exporters. In the near term, world supply disruptions are more likely to cause domestic price shocks than actual shortages. Such shocks would affect both GNP and the distribution of wealth. They could increase unemployment and accelerate the obsolescence of energy-using capital stock. The adjustment costs of short-term fuel switching and long-term fuel substitution would fall to all sectors as inputs were reallocated to match changes in the demand for goods. Caught by surprise, owners of energy-consuming capital stock (vehicles, boilers, etc.) would be forced to either absorb the price increase or to buy new stock before the useful life of the old stock ended. Chronic oil and gas import dependence would increase the transfer of wealth abroad, perhaps retarding long-term capital formation and "factor productivity" at home. With a swollen oil-driven trade deficit, the United States could also watch its currency depreciate and the real cost of non-oil imports rise as a result (Toman, 1991). On top of these effects are the military costs of securing oil-transportation routes (Koplow, 1993) and the less tangible constraints imposed on U.S. foreign policy.

Through renewable energy development, oil dependence could be reduced, particularly if electricity were to play a larger role in transportation or if renewably-generated hydrogen were to replace oil on a large scale. Alone, the use of renewable energy for the "end uses" considered here will make a much more modest contribution to energy security. Nationally, petroleum supplies only about 5 percent of electricity generation and 15 percent of space heating (EIA, 1993),[11] so energy-security benefits of switching to renewables to provide these energy services are much smaller than they are for finding substitutes for transport fuel. But even the benefits associated with reducing oil dependence for electricity generation and space heating probably won't enter into energy supply decisions because oil prices don't fully reflect the social risks of oil dependence.

Of the various policy options for addressing energy-security risks, diversifying supply sources is one of the most robust. Unlike measures designed primarily to reduce the risks of dependence on Middle East imports (strategic releases of government oil reserves, subsidies to domestic oil production, or the diversification of world oil supplies), the development of oil substitutes reduces a much broader class of social costs imposed on the economy (Bohi and Toman, 1992).

Equitable Distribution of Economic Benefits

The environmental, security, and sustainability benefits of using renewables accrue broadly across the country. Both inter-generational equity and intra-generational equity in the distribution of income and jobs relative to the prevailing energy supply mix are served by renewable energy development. Moreover, the local income and employment benefits of renewables tend to be more evenly dispersed across the country than those related to fossil-fuel cycles.

The Geographic Distribution of Benefits

In general, fossil-fuel production is more regionally concentrated than renewable energy production, partly because oil and gas reserves are often found together while wind, insolation, and other renewable energy flows aren't clustered. *(See Table II-6.)* But though 39 states derive 3 or more percent of their energy needs from renewables, the potential for dispersed renewable energy production is far greater than current production patterns suggest.

Although the regional patterns of fossil-fuel production are unlikely to change greatly, substantial renewable resources can be tapped in locations where production is currently low. Potential crop biomass resources are spread throughout the North Central region, forest biomass in the Southeast and Northwest, hydrothermal in the West, wind on both coasts and in the North Central and Great Plains regions, and direct insolation (for concentrating collectors) in the Southwest. Diffuse solar radiation (for flat-plate collectors and passive solar gain) could be harnessed cost-effectively across much of the country. Other geothermal technologies could potentially produce geothermal heat in several regions. Overall, as Figures II-2 to II-7 show, virtually all states have potentially substantial renewable resources.

The economic benefits of renewables are distributed in much the same geographical pattern as the resources themselves—certainly not the case with fossil fuels. Energy production with local renewable resources allows communities to add value to the local economy by stemming losses of income or employment. If, for instance, a utility operates both wind machines and fossil-fuel-fired plants and the cost of the energy generated is the same, with the wind plant dollars do not leave the service area to pay for imported fuel, while with the fossil-fuel generating facility, they do.[12] Of course, the "value-added" to the local economy from wind development would be even greater if the turbines were fabricated locally too. For end-use applications of renewables, such as solar water heaters, installation and servicing creates local employment.

Of course, choosing a wind or other renewable energy plant means foregoing fossil-fuel production. But while economic dislocations from a major shift to renewables need to be addressed, the fossil-fuel industry's structure limits local economic benefits anyway. In general, most of the income from fossil-fuel development flows to those who own the resource. Coal royalties, for example, go to a relatively small number of mine owners. Moreover, since

Table II-6. 1990 Concentration of National Production of Fossil Fuels and Renewables

Energy Source	Percentage Produced in Five Top-Producing States
Coal (short tons)	63% (WY, KY, WV, PA, IL)[1]
Natural Gas (Cubic Feet)	83% (TX, LA, OK, NM WY)[2]
Crude Oil (Barrels)	75% (TX, AK, CA, LA, OK)[3]
All Renewables (Btus)	46% (WA, CA, OR, GA, NY)[4]
Electric Renewables (Btus)	65% (WA, CA, OR, NY, AL)[5]
Non-Hydro Renewables (Btus)	37% (CA, GA, AL, NC, LA)[6]

Notes:
1. EIA, 1990.
2. U.S. DOE et al., 1991b.
3. U.S. DOE, 1990.
4. Rader et al., 1990.
5. Ibid.
6. Ibid.

coal is produced mainly in areas with modest electrical needs, most coal is exported, and local employment income from coal extraction pales besides the owners' take.

The Distribution of Economic Benefits Among Income Levels

Energy projects can generate economic benefits that affect people at different income levels differently. Benefits arise from job creation, shifts to higher-paying occupations, and the disposition of profits, rents, and royalties from resource extraction. Although each energy project is unique in this respect, renewable energy technologies appear to offer economic benefits that are relatively dispersed across income levels.

The economic value of employment stimulated by an energy project depends on workers' previous employment status. Since this is difficult to ascertain, job creation is often used as a proxy for

Figure II-2: Renewable Energy as a Fraction of State Energy Consumption

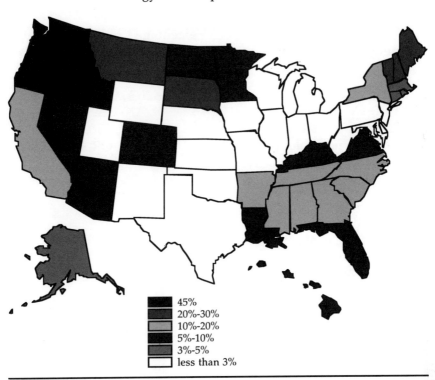

- 45%
- 20%-30%
- 10%-20%
- 5%-10%
- 3%-5%
- less than 3%

Source: Rader et al., 1990

economic value. Past studies generally show net employment gains from renewable energy scenarios, thanks to both the high labor intensity of renewables and to the re-spending of energy savings from cost-effective renewable investment (Muller et al., 1992). In one input/output study (Council on Economic Priorities, 1979), regional labor years per million dollars of expenditure were estimated to be 41 for a solar and conservation scenario,[13] compared to 17 for a nuclear scenario. The same study found solar hot water installation more labor-intensive than the addition of passive solar elements to buildings. Another study also concluded that energy

Figure II-3: Conventional Hydroelectric Power, Developed and Undeveloped

By Water Resources Regions

Million Kilowatts

■ Developed □ Undeveloped

Source: Federal Energy Regulatory Commission, 1988

scenarios based largely on renewables are more labor-intensive than scenarios emphasizing competing energy sources. Total national energy-sector employment increased along with the percentage of total energy provided through solar technologies, even taking account of other energy sector losses. Because solar technologies are modular, their use also stabilized local employment over time more than in boom-and-bust scenarios involving the construction of a single large electric power plant (Schiffman and D'Alessio, 1983).

Figure II-4: Wind Resources Sites of 13 MPH and Higher

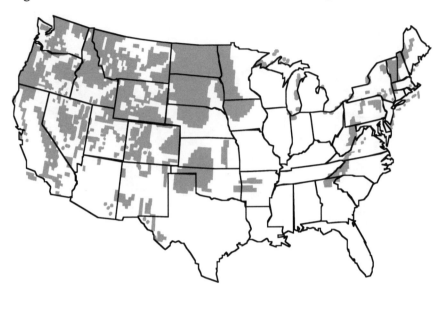

Source: National Renewable Energy Laboratory

Recent studies corroborate these early results. In one (ASE, AGA, and SEIA, 1992), the employment effects of a business-as-usual energy future are compared with those associated with a scenario emphasizing reliance on natural gas, energy efficiency, and renewables. Nationally, the net increase in jobs from the alternative energy future ranges from 83,000 to 152,000 for the year 2000. Another recent study found that energy-efficiency investments, by lowering energy users' utility bills, create more jobs than investments in conventional power plants. Increases in employment certainly reflect the relative labor intensity of efficiency measures, but a dominant factor is that energy consumers spend their utility bill savings on other goods and services (Geller, deCicco, and Laitner, 1992). For the same reason, demand-side renewable energy measures are likely to result in net employment gains.

Figure II-5: Biomass Resource Availability

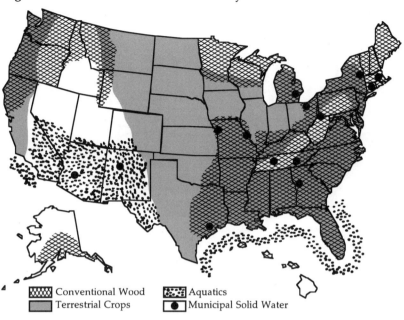

▨ Conventional Wood		▒ Aquatics	
▨ Terrestrial Crops		● Municipal Solid Water	

Biomass Resources are Widespread

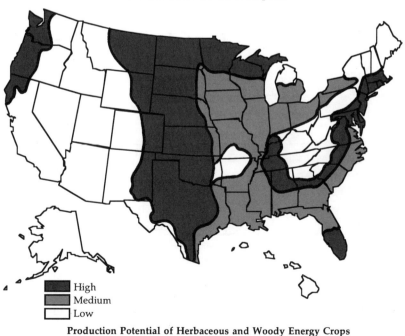

■ High	
▨ Medium	
□ Low	

Production Potential of Herbaceous and Woody Energy Crops

Source: National Renewable Energy Laboratory

51

Figure II-6: Geothermal Resource Availability

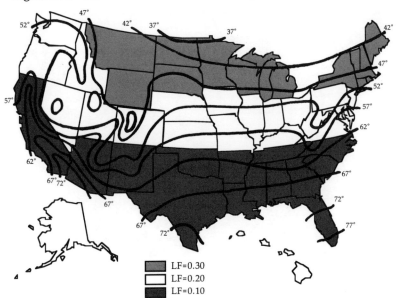

Average Ground Water Temperature and Heating Load Factors for Heat Pump Analysis

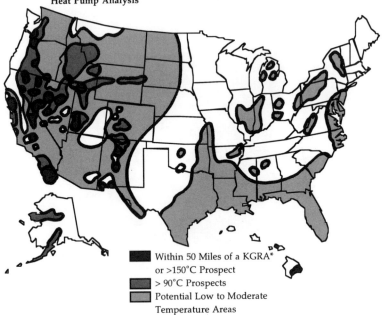

Known and Potential Hydrothermal Resources

* Known Geothermal Resource Areas

Source: National Renewable Energy Laboratory

Figure II-7: Annual Average Daily Global Solar Radiation on a South Facing Surface (Tilt=Latitude)

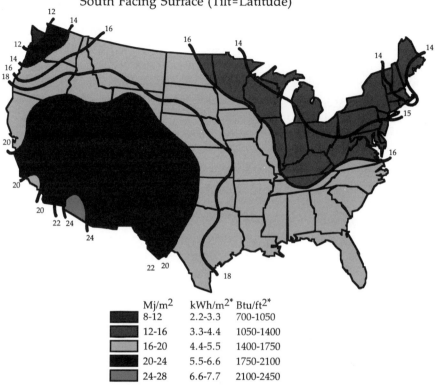

Mj/m^2	kWh/m^{2*}	Btu/ft^{2*}
8-12	2.2-3.3	700-1050
12-16	3.3-4.4	1050-1400
16-20	4.4-5.5	1400-1750
20-24	5.5-6.6	1750-2100
24-28	6.6-7.7	2100-2450

*Approximate Values
Note: Numbered contours represent Mj/m^2

Photovoltaic (solar cell) arrays should be oriented for maximum exposure to solar radiation throughout the year. A tilt angle equal to the site latitude is recommended for fixed position collectors (e.g., for Denver: Latitude = 40°, Tilt angle = 40°).

Source: National Renewable Energy Laboratory

Besides these "scenario" analyses, other studies have compared national and local employment creation per dollar expended or energy unit generated. Comparing (within state) employee years per unit of energy output for several energy technologies (New York State Energy Office, 1992), researchers for the state of New York found that renewables tend to generate more employment per unit of energy output than either fossil fuels or demand-side management measures and to outperform fossil-fuel technologies in terms of employment per dollar expended. As Table II-7 shows, renewables have relatively low fuel costs and high O&M costs as a percentage of total costs. In contrast, for a natural gas plant, 74 percent of total cost is from fuel expenditures. Since expenditures on fuel generate less local employment than other cost components do, the natural gas combined-cycle plant contributes the fewest jobs per dollar expended.[14]

Two Wisconsin case studies of the effects of a high-use renewables scenario on employment came to similar conclusions. In one, displacing 810 MW of fossil-fuel capacity with renewables would create 700 net jobs. In both studies, economic benefits result from displacing imported fossil fuels and generating local value-added activities (Brower et al., 1993; Clemmer, 1993).

To see how equitably income from energy production is distributed also requires tracing royalties. The key questions are which income classes own the resource and how resource-extraction sites are distributed geographically (Rose et al., 1982). Since renewable energy flows tend to be diffuse, royalty income from these flows could be broadly distributed among resource owners. Over time, renewables also generate a relatively constant stream of royalty payments. In contrast, a coal mine or oil well generates income only as long as the stock is worth extracting.

Banking on Renewables in Uncertain Times

The environmental, economic, security, and equity benefits of renewables would be of little concern to public policy-makers if market prices fully reflected these benefits. For then, renewables would be taken into account in all private decisions concerning energy supply and demand. But since market prices reflect much narrower concerns, renewables' market penetration pales beside its potential.

Even if market prices reflected the known social costs of energy-production activities, they might not fully incorporate the risk-reducing benefits of renewables. If these benefits are considered, the rationale for going beyond the business-as-usual rate of

Table II-7. Labor Intensity and Percent of Total Expenditures Allocated to O & M and Fuel by Energy Resource

Energy Resource Alternative	Percent of Total Expenditures		Employee Years per 10 GWh
	O&M (percent)	Fuel (percent)	
Natural Gas Combined Cycle	11	66	2.63
Wind	22	0	6.41
Urban Wood Waste	30	5	5.80
Photovoltaic	13	0	22.31
Small Hydro	7	0	7.21
MSW w/o Tipping Fees	34	0	14.82
DSM	1	0	5.05
Life Extension Coal to Coal w/SO$_2$ removal	37	36	2.86
Integrated Coal Gasification Combination Cycle (IGCC)	18	25	3.47
Repowering Existing Coal to IGCC	24	32	2.83

Source: New York State Energy Office, 1992.

market penetration grows stronger, even if known costs and benefits don't justify the move. For example, avoiding potentially irreversible ecological damages and other effects from fossil-fuel emissions (such as CO_2, NO_x, and SO_x) requires displacing fossil-fuel consumption *before* some critical threshold is reached.

·Uncertainties surrounding some types of risk (such as the extent of damages from climate change) could be dispelled or confirmed in the near future as scientific understanding deepens. But our country's energy infrastructure responds very slowly to new information. Indeed, a premium should be put on improving society's flexibility in its energy-technology choices. Meeting a utility's need for 500 MW in 2000 with a series of small renewable generators allows more flexibility to respond to new information than building a single 500-MW fossil fuel plant does. More generally, every time a new generation of fossil-fuel-burning power plants and the associated infrastructure is built, as will happen in the next decade, society commits itself to 40 or more years of CO_2 emissions. Unfortunately, without changes in public policy, near-term energy-supply decisions will not reflect the importance of staying flexible enough to respond to future developments.

III.

REFORMING ENERGY-PRICE SIGNALS

Of the many social benefits from renewables summarized in the previous chapter, environmental protection has received the most attention in attempts to influence private energy decisions through "full cost pricing." Though differentially increasing the cost of energy sources to reflect their environmental risks is conceptually straightforward, experts are divided over both the best analytical techniques for calculating the monetary values of environmental effects and the most appropriate tools for implementing them. But the U.S. energy supply mix is distorted by government policy as well as by market failures, and reforming these policies—whether taxes, regulations, or subsidies—is the best way to remove these distortions.

Internalizing Social Costs

If the goal is to get utilities and energy users to incorporate the environmental costs of various modes of energy production into their decisions, several policy alternatives are available. Each has advantages and disadvantages with respect to cost effectiveness, accuracy, administrative ease, clarity, comprehensiveness, and responsiveness to new information. Also, as the following brief review indicates, some policy options are designed to reduce emissions directly, while others reduce reliance on polluting energy sources. (Additional detail can be found in the large literature on this topic. *See*, for example, Burtraw and Krupnick, 1992; Oak Ridge National Laboratory and Resources for the Future, 1992.)

Policy Tools For Reducing Emissions

• *Pollution Taxes* Recouping the environmental costs of energy production through taxes promotes more cost-effective pollution reductions than most other strategies. By creating an economic incentive to reduce pollution, taxes do not restrict the range of possible abatement technologies or responses, unlike many pollution control programs. Taxes encourage each pollution source to find the least expensive means of lowering emissions. Taxes also encourage industry to continue developing pollution-reducing technologies. Taxing carbon-dioxide emissions, for example, would cost far less than regulatory approaches that reduce carbon by the same amount (Dower and Zimmerman, 1992). In addition, pollution taxes can be applied at the beginning of the fuel cycle so that utilities and energy users incorporate environmental costs in all downstream decisions.

Given these advantages, why haven't pollution tax strategies been widely applied to energy production (or any other pollution source) in the United States? One concern is that taxes do not directly control the amount of pollution produced. Many advocates of conventional pollution control programs prefer the certainty of regulations that set a specific limit to the amount of allowable pollution. Of course, pollution taxes can be designed to meet any pollution control target. This is achieved, however, by increasing or lowering the tax, not the quantity of pollution. Tax-based pollution control strategies do, in this sense, involve a trade-off between cost-effectiveness and the certainty with which environmental goals are met. It is important to note, however, that this concern is less important for pollutants that are already subject to conventional pollution control requirements or those that are less damaging to health or the environment on a pound for pound basis.

• *Tradable Permits* An alternative to environmental taxes is to establish a cap under which emissions can be traded. In this approach, individual sources of a pollutant might be assigned an allowable emissions level based on a national target. Only energy users with emissions large enough to be regulated (utilities and industries) are affected and, unlike taxes, this approach has no direct effects on individual consumers. Firms that can cheaply reduce emissions below their allocation could sell their pollution reductions to other companies or utilities that can stay within bounds only at high cost. The net effect is the same as under pollution taxes: a pollution target is achieved at the lowest possible cost. Emission-trading programs with a cap on both new and existing emission sources would reduce pollution faster than approaches affecting only acquisition decisions about new resources.

How tradable permit systems are implemented determines how various regions, technologies, and industries are affected. One scheme, the offset, allows a firm to fund measures that reduce its net emissions by a quantifiable amount, even if the measures aren't part of the firm's operations. If the goal is reducing carbon-dioxide emissions, offset measures might include fuel switching, carbon fixation, energy conservation, and the use of renewables. (The 1990 Clean Air Act Amendments include a modest provision designating renewables and energy-efficiency measures as potential offsets for SO_2 reductions.) Renewables may work well in offset programs since emission reductions related to expanding their use are relatively easy to quantify, though shutting down inefficient fossil-fuel burning equipment has been a more common form of offset in programs to date.

Tradable permits' main advantage over taxes is greater certainty about resulting emissions levels. While tax rates can be ratcheted up or down as needed, responding to the new tax rates can be expensive if capital investments have already been targeted to reducing emissions to the initially desired level. Also, for pollutants whose damages vary regionally, tax rates based on national average damage costs may be less efficient than permits.

Emission-trading schemes work best when pollution sources are numerous and fairly homogeneous and when policy-makers are relatively certain about the level of pollution control needed. But, for some pollutants—CO_2 among them—these conditions do not hold, so it's difficult to set targets and allocate permits. Still, emission-trading schemes make sense if verifying emission reductions is of primary importance.

It is important to consider who will pay or have responsibility for the initial pollution control requirements. Under most emission trading proposals, existing sources of pollution are granted the right to continue to pollute, at some reduced level, at no cost. Pollution taxes, however, must be paid on every unit of pollution—there is no free level.

• *Regulatory Approaches*. The most common approach at the federal and state level for addressing environmental risks is to require energy producers to use specified technologies to reduce pollution or to meet specific emissions targets. The appeals of these "command and control" approaches to internalizing environmental risks have been enforceability and dependability. But rarely do they control pollution at the lowest possible cost, and the economic disadvantages of these programs—such as forcing all power plants to use the same control strategy—are well documented. Command-and-control regulation makes the most sense in attempts to control particularly dangerous pollutants or prevent irreversible environmental impacts.

Policies that Influence Energy Supply Choices

Another set of policy tools seeks to directly influence energy-supply choices. If the primary objective is to internalize the environmental costs of different energy sources, these policies tend to be less cost-effective than those that aim to reduce pollution. However, they may serve other social objectives.

• *Energy Taxes* Depending on how it is crafted, an energy tax may affect energy choices in much the same way that a pollution tax does. For example, an *ad valorem* tax raises the cost of different energy sources in proportion to their pre-tax costs while a Btu tax raises the cost of energy sources in proportion to their energy content. At current market prices, a Btu tax looks more like a pollution tax in its effects than an *ad valorem* tax does because a fuel's energy content is more closely correlated with pollution than is its price. For instance, the Btu tax results in a greater increase in the relative cost of coal than does the *ad valorem* tax designed to raise the same level of revenues. (Neither, however, is as effective as taxing pollution directly.)

In early 1993, the Clinton administration proposed to tax the Btu content of fossil[15] and nuclear fuels and hydropower (based on the average fossil-fuel input to generate equivalent electricity). Other renewable energy sources were exempted. As initially proposed, this tax would have modestly increased the cost of conventional fuels relative to that of renewable electricity (other than hydropower) and renewable thermal energy. In this respect, the tax reflected some of the social costs of fossil fuels that are not reflected in market prices. *(See Chapter II.)* Residential natural gas prices would have increased 4 percent, residential electricity 3 percent, and home heating oil 8 percent. At these levels, however, the tax would have had little direct effect on emission levels, reducing conventional energy consumption in the year 2000 by only 2 percent as a combined result of price-induced conservation and fuel switching (Laitner, 1993). The administration's proposal did not address all of the social costs of current energy-production patterns that should be internalized through higher taxes or other means. A much larger Btu tax would have been needed to reduce emissions significantly and prompt utilities and consumers to make different energy choices. Moreover, to affect such decisions, any energy tax must be collected at the point where energy supply decisions are made—a point of contention with the Administration's proposal before it was withdrawn.[16]

• *Environmental Adders* Consistent with their mandate to protect ratepayers' interests, state public utility commissions (PUCs) are raising legitimate concerns about the environmental implications of operating existing plants, the need for new plants, and the mix of resources used to fuel new plants. PUCs across the United States are experimenting with alternative policy instruments aimed at forcing utilities to internalize the environmental and, possibly, other social costs associated with different energy sources being considered for use. In some states, environmental costs are treated as qualitative weights during resource planning or acquisition. In others, external costs must be quantified. As of 1992, for example, some nine PUCs had either adopted rules for monetizing environmental externalities in utility resource planning or were in the process of doing so (Hamrin and Rader, 1993).

Of these options, the use of quantitative adders has been the most attention-getting and controversial. The idea is to add cents/kWh charges based on environmental costs to the estimated private costs of all generation alternatives that a utility is evaluating for possible acquisition. Although qualitative approaches to environmental externalities don't impart a false sense of precision the way adders might, adders may be a less subjective decision-making tool. In any case, imposing either adders or weights potentially affects the ranking of resource options for planning purposes, though utilities rarely add such charges to customer rates or to the amounts paid to resource developers. To the extent that resource acquisitions differ from what they would be under purely private costing, however, customer rates will eventually rise under any of these options.

Without question, imposing quantitative adders can change a utility's incentives to make long-term capital investments. But how effective adders are in achieving environmental objectives depends on how they are implemented. Without complementary policies, adders can give a comparative advantage to existing power plants (most of which are dirtier than new projects), public utility projects, and industrial sources of the same emissions. On the other hand, because adders affect only marginal investment decisions, externalities can be internalized gradually and values fine-tuned as scientific understanding of environmental damages improves. To curb emissions from existing power-plants, the priority system by which a utility's plants are dispatched would also need to change: sole emphasis on private operating costs would have to shift to a dual emphasis on both operating and environmental costs. With this so-called social cost dispatch, ratepayers would pay prices that correctly reflect the full costs of current energy consumption. A wild card, however, is the result if rate increases encourage large industrial customers to leave the grid and generate their own electricity: total emissions could go up or down.

In general, policy tools that directly affect environmental costs (such as a pollution tax) are less blunt than those (such as a Btu tax) that affect energy supply choices. Of those tools that affect energy choices, an across-the-board Btu tax is more comprehensive than the adder approach.

Estimating Environmental Costs

Many of the policy options for internalizing environmental damages require PUCs to assign monetary values to the damages. To the extent that social costs have already been partially internalized as a result of twenty years of regulating energy-production facilities, private energy markets already register some of the environmental benefits of using renewables. But since environmental damage remains significant, both the costs of these residual environmental damages and the savings from avoiding future environmental risks should ideally be reflected in the cost of all energy sources.

As shown in Table III-1, depending on the combustion technology, conventional environmental costs associated with operating fossil fuel power plants range from an estimated $0.001 to $0.10/delivered kWh. Ranges for solar, wind, and biomass (other than Municipal Solid Waste) technologies are much lower. External costs from large hydro facilities can be quite high, depending on location (Ottinger et al., 1990). But the average difference between the environmental costs of electricity production from renewables (solar, wind, and biomass) and nonrenewables is substantial—in some cases, great enough to change the ranking of energy options, depending on where facilities are located and how costs are internalized.

Table III-1. External Costs from Electric Generation Technologies ($1990 cents/kWh)

Technology	Range[1]
Combustion Turbine: Gas	0.1 – 6.0
Combustion Turbine: Oil	0.3 –10.3
Coal	0.6 –10.0
Nuclear	<0.1 –13.0[2]
Photovoltaic	0.0 – 0.4
Wind	0.0 – 0.1
Biomass	0.0 – 0.7
MSW	(3.7)–48.2
Geothermal	0 –<0.1

Notes:
1. Ranges based on data cited in Chupka and Howarth, 1992.
2. Upper end of range based on Hohmeyer, 1992b.

For several reasons, these estimates should be treated with caution. First, some estimates are based on the cost (dollars per ton) of controlling various pollutants, which may be a poor proxy for the damage associated with one more ton of pollution from a given source. Such estimates would approximate true social costs only if the marginal social costs equalled the benefits of compliance exactly, which is highly unlikely considering that environmental effects from other, uncontrolled points in the fuel cycle are not fully considered and damages are generally location-specific. For these reasons, in any given case, control costs could be more or less than actual damages (Burtraw and Krupnick, 1992).

Even estimates based on known damages can be problematic. If state and federal environmental regulations, such as the Clean Air Act Amendments, aren't taken into account when environmental costs are calculated, pollution-reduction benefits of renewables will probably be overestimated. On the other hand, because complete fuel-cycle analyses and the effects of energy use on climate are typically left out of the energy-cost calculus, estimated cost differences between renewables and other energy sources tend to be conservative. In fact, damage values from currently unregulated environmental impacts—among them, damages from carbon-dioxide emissions and such air-borne toxics as mercury—are unlikely to be anything close to zero.

By any reckoning, the total environmental effects and associated costs of using different fuels remain uncertain. With various analysts pegging the appropriate environmental charge for coal at anywhere from 21 percent to 1,025 percent of its market price (Viscusi et al., 1993), how are regulators supposed to estimate environmental cost values? Certainly, estimating residual damages directly is conceptually preferable to basing estimates on control costs. But though market-related damages (such as crop losses) can be readily estimated, procedures for estimating most non-market costs (such as the loss of ecological diversity or an increase in respiratory ailments) are far more difficult and controversial—partly because ordinary people's sense of which environmental risks are most serious often differs from what experts think. Choosing some positive value for the social costs of an energy supply option is an analytic improvement over assuming they amount to zero only if the chosen value is closer to the actual value than is zero.

Disagreements over what cost values are appropriate persist, and the use of environmental adders has been challenged with mixed results. The controversy has led the Massachusetts PUC to allow power developers to use emission offsets, such as tree planting, to reduce the cents/kWh values that they would otherwise have to apply to polluting energy sources. Other states have decided not to require such estimates, but nevertheless recognize ratepayers' preference for some electric generation options over others.[17]

If energy consumers' changing environmental priorities are ignored, a utility's generation mix may become out of sync with ratepayers' desires for environmental protection. To make sure that this doesn't happen, PUCs have several options. One is to implicitly incorporate externalities into ratemaking by allowing higher rates of return or granting related incentives for acquiring environmentally benign resources (Cohen et al., 1990). Another is to require utilities to include specified quantities of renewables in resource acquisitions. *(See Chapter IV.)*

A few PUCs require utilities to account for the financial risks associated with predictable future environmental regulations to the extent they already do for uncertainties surrounding the costs of future fuel, O&M, and other factors related to generation choices. Even though environmental control is more likely to increase than decrease in the future,[18] utilities probably don't consider this probability fully when making long-term energy-supply choices. If utilities knew that over the 40-year life of a power plant regulators might challenge rate increases resulting from compliance with CO_2-reduction requirements, they might choose more environmentally benign generation options. California's PUC stated in 1992 that utilities should purchase fossil-fuel-based generating capacity only if the supplier demonstrates that it can bear any future costs associated with meeting carbon-emission-control requirements, and Wisconsin and Texas may be following suit.[19]

Implications for Renewable Energy and Environmental Policy

Incorporating environmental costs into energy prices is an *environmental* policy, not a renewable energy development policy, and internalizing environmental costs alone is unlikely to enable the United States to cost-effectively overcome other barriers to deployment of renewables. Nor will internalizing environmental costs always change energy choices. According to one recent projection, if all states applied adders comparable to those used in Massachusetts, national renewable electricity production would by 2030 be roughly double that of the base case (Wood and Naill, 1992). But in another study, when environmental costs are incorporated into utility-investment decisions, renewables' share of the utility's generating mix increases in only one out of five simulated scenarios: when carbon-dioxide is taxed at $100/ton and NO_x and SO_2 are taxed as well (Palmer and Krupnick, 1991). Further, since various renewable electric technologies have differing pollution-prevention potential, internalizing environmental costs would favor some renewables more than others. For example, a carbon tax of $50/metric ton would add an estimated 1.3 cents/kWh to the average value of windpower and hydropower, but only 0.8 cents/kWh to the value of geothermal generation (Chupka and Howarth, 1992). When ranking energy sources according to social cost, renewables' environmental advantages are most likely to alter decisions if they are already almost competitive with traditional energy sources.

Still, processes for internalizing such costs can be improved in several ways. First, the best available cost estimates and implementation tools should be used to internalize environmental costs, regardless of how individual energy technologies fare in the comparison. Estimation techniques must be refined so that states can periodically update estimates of external costs as new scientific and economic valuation data become available and feedback from the implementation of current environmental regulations accumulates. Methods for adapting cost values from other studies may be defensible when used to rank future electricity-supply options, but they are not accurate enough to be used to change the order in which existing plants are dispatched (Krupnick, 1993). Second, monetary estimates should be developed and applied only to those environmental impacts for which data and analytical procedures are relatively well-established. Third, states should better coordinate utility regulation with other state and federal environmental regulation. In particular, state utility regulators must consider how state policies—say the imposition of adders—could interact with existing federal environmental regulation (such as the Clean Air Act Amendments).

The division of responsibility between federal and state governments for implementing policy tools also needs to change. Even though states have been most active to date, the federal government should take the lead in enacting policies—especially those that would, like a national carbon tax, internalize the costs of transboundary pollution. Considering that the environmental effects from power production often cross state boundaries (as do electricity grids), the equity and cost-effectiveness of state-level approaches to pollution control is open to question. Some states are net contributors of acid rain precursors, for example, while others receive more than they produce. Moreover, each state and utility is responsible for only a tiny fraction of global greenhouse gas emissions, so unilateral PUC action to reduce these emissions would not materially benefit state residents. Then too, unilateral state action could create incentives for electricity-intensive industries to relocate. If PUCs continue to internalize environmental costs, utilities and their fuel suppliers will have to contend with varying state approaches and values.

Barring a national approach, regional coordination should supplement state-by-state approaches. Regional power planning, for example, might allow neighboring states to better harmonize the values of their environmental adders. For controlling existing transboundary pollution sources, emission offsets could be structured to be cost-effective, as long as offset costs are justified by benefits to state residents.

States should also ensure that policies for reducing emission levels from current and future plants' generating capacity are consistent with each other. For example, cost-internalization policies should take into account the environmental costs of operating existing power plants. The best option here is a federal pollution tax, but extending adders to cover existing plants is an alternative worth considering. (Including coverage of existing plants in cost-internalization policies would probably increase the near-term share of renewables in a utility's generating supply mix more than including only marginal capacity additions would (Wood and Naill, 1992).

In any such effort, coordination is key. If they try to force utilities to take environmental costs into account, PUCs should make their efforts consistent with environmental regulations applied to the utility, industrial, and transportation sectors. And the federal government should give states technical assistance so that they can better coordinate their policies with federal environmental policies.

Reforming Energy Subsidies

In addition to correcting market failure, getting prices right also requires examining government subsidies that favor some energy technologies over others and getting rid of subsidies that work against national energy policies.

Estimating Existing Subsidies

Depending on how they are measured, recent estimates of direct federal subsidies to the energy sector range from about $5 billion to $36 billion per year. *(See Table III-2.)*[20] Nonrenewable energy sources receive the lion's share of total subsidies. But there is no standard way to interpret these totals. How much a subsidy may drain the federal budget, for example, doesn't necessarily correlate with its impact on energy producers. As a percentage of total sales, direct subsidies appear small. However, the subsidy rate (the ratio of the subsidy to the total value of domestic shipments) enjoyed by energy industries is among the highest for all U.S. industrial sectors (Kaminow, 1989). Moreover, the cumulative effects of subsidies over time on energy production and price may differ from their effects registered in a single year (Spewak, 1988). Indeed, the disproportionately heavy subsidies received by fossil and nuclear technologies over the past 20 years, for example, in part accounts for their low cost relative to some renewable technologies today (U.S. GAO, 1993). In the case of biomass energy crops, existing subsidies favor both food and conventional energy production.

The "subsidy intensity" (amount of subsidy per unit of energy) of individual renewable and nonrenewable energy sources varies widely and shows no clear pattern. For 1989 electric generation,

Table III-2. Federal Subsidies by Energy Type ($ Millions) from Two Recent Studies

Energy Type	Alliance to Save Energy (ASE) Estimate for 1989 ($1989)[1]	EIA Estimate for FY92 ($1992)[2]
Oil	5,469–8,758	-2,131
Gas	2,149–4,275	1,903
Coal	5,557–8,043	2,151
Nuclear[3]	5,453–10,992	1,295
Efficiency	567–983	635
Total Renewables	1,823–2,806	1,014
Hydroelectricity	377–623	Not reported
Total Non-hydro Renewables	1,446–2,183	Not reported
Nonethanol Biomass	260–382	Not reported
Solar	158–176	Not reported
Wind	39–64	Not reported
Geothermal	158–254	Not reported
Ethanol	534–879	Not reported
Waste-to-Energy	274–404	Not reported
Total for All Energy Sources	**21,018–35,857**	**4,867**

Notes:
1. Range reflects direct government costs (low) and value to recipients (high) of all subsidies affecting the energy sector (Koplow, 1993).
2. Valued on the basis of federal budget outlays to the energy sector (EIA, 1992d). To make energy categories consistent with ASE data, electricity subsidies were prorated among sources of generation based on 1992 fuel consumption data.
3. Includes fission and fusion.

coal was subsidized at an estimated 0.48 cents/kWh, fission at 2.00 cents/kWh, and natural gas at 0.37 cents/kWh (Koplow, 1993). Renewables display a similarly wide range, with wind at 0.34 cents/kWh and geothermal at 1.95 cents/kWh.[21]

In terms of the relative attractiveness of current investments in renewable versus fossil fuel energy, however, the picture looks different. Even small differences in rates of return can affect the relative attractiveness of investments—and thus of energy technology choices—at the margin. Although subsidies are not limited to tax incentives, many provisions in the federal tax code increase the relative attractiveness of investing in nonrenewable energy sources. *(See Box III-1.)* Because some renewables require relatively great amounts of capital and land to develop, their property, sales, and corporate tax liability is commensurately high *(See,* for example, Lotker, 1991). Several tax breaks for fossil-fuel producers grow as energy prices drop, but none for renewable energy developers do. Further, the requirements that oil and gas investors have to follow when computing minimum tax liability are less restrictive than those for investors in renewable energy. And the expensing of intangible drilling costs associated with oil and gas properties is allowed provided that deductions don't exceed 65 percent of net income from such properties in a given year. Those who invest in renewables other than geothermal resources enjoy no such comparable deduction.

Subsidies undoubtedly affect our current energy mix and associated infrastructure, as well as the expected viability of future alternatives. While the importance of subsidies to particular energy sources varies according to how the subsidies are measured, it is clear that a free market in energy does not exist. Moreover, the disparity in subsidies that favor well-established energy sources reflects the long time such subsidies have had to accumulate more than it does current national policy.

Reforming the Tax Code

There are two fundamental policy options for remedying tax code biases: create countervailing subsidies for renewable energy or minimize subsidies for conventional energy sources. Unless the point is to achieve other social objectives (such as environmental

Box III-1. Tax Provisions Favoring Fossil Fuels

Capital Versus Operating Costs in Energy Production and Consumption. The high capital intensity and low operating costs of most renewable technologies compared to fossil fuel technologies mean that any tax provisions favoring operating costs over capital costs lower the cost of energy from fossil fuels relative to that from renewable energy applications. For example, business can deduct fuel costs as operating expenses from taxes owed. And while the natural gas purchased by a utility for a gas-fired plant is generally exempt from sales taxes, developers of a renewable energy project pay sales taxes on equipment they buy to construct the plant (Lotker, 1991).

Investor-owned utilities can also subtract the cost of fuel as an operating expense before calculating federal income taxes on revenues. For electric utilities, fuel expensing can result in substantial reductions in tax liability, estimated at about $11 billion nationally for the utility industry in 1990 (U.S. DOE, 1991c, unpublished data).

A commercial enterprise can fully charge all fuel costs against taxable income, while the only capital costs that can be deducted are for depreciation and interest payments. For homeowners, capital equipment adds to the taxable value of real property and replaces fuel purchases that are subject only to the sales tax at the state or local level. In other words, any increase in property taxes can offset part of the fuel cost savings. Of course, if renewable energy equipment in new home construction is financed through a home mortgage, incremental interest payments are tax-deductible.

Exploration, Development, and Production Incentives. Tax provisions help sustain advanced technologies in the oil and gas industries when energy prices are low. The rate of oil and gas production incentives, including the Section-29 production credit, the Section-56h energy preference adjustment, and the Section-43 enhanced oil recovery credit, vary with energy

(continued on next page)

Box III-1. *(continues)*

prices. If oil prices fell below $28/barrel in the prior calendar year, deductions for certain drilling costs are increased. Also, 50-percent depletion on production of marginal drilling properties is allowed in computing the minimum tax liability to the extent that the additional deductions do not reduce tax liability by more than 40 percent, and in 1992, federal legislation increased the returns on capital investment in new oil and gas wells by ending alternative minimum tax (AMT) liabilities for independent producers. The coal industry also receives a percentage depletion on coal mines, and it is eligible for the Section-29 Production Credit for gasified coal and gas produced from coal seams.

Tax provisions also reduce the financial burden on the fossil-fuel industry of complying with environmental regulation. Currently, there is a tax incentive under Section 169 for installing pollution-control equipment: equipment used in connection with facilities in operation before 1976 can be amortized in just five years. At least eight states provide five-year accelerated depreciation for pollution-control facilities (Totten and Settina, 1993).

protection or wealth redistribution), the goal of energy tax code reform should be minimizing interference in energy-investment choices.[22] This approach would reduce the economic efficiency losses associated with taxation (Musgrave and Musgrave, 1989) and create more accurate energy-price signals for efficient energy use. Particularly important is minimizing the tax-code disparity between capital-intensive and fuel cost-intensive technologies such as fuel-expensing. But since fuel-expensing is an established practice that business is sure to defend, it should be phased down to some percentage—allowing ample lead time for investors to change course. (Precedents exist: other expense deductions have been limited in recent years.)

While the subsidy reduction approach is politically difficult, it has several advantages. Minimizing tax subsidies would save policy-makers the trouble of calculating, case by case, the value of offsetting tax provisions (which may create their own distortions). To quantify existing inequities, the full fuel-cycle tax impact on each competing energy source would have to be measured, perhaps using as a yardstick total tax liability per unit of energy produced relative to the unit cost of energy. Such analyses must then be replicated to account for the varying effects of the federal, state, and local tax codes on specific energy choices and specific energy users (landlords, utilities, etc.). Even then, interpreting all resulting differences in tax liability (including among different renewables) as inequities would be contentious because of the very different operating and economic characteristics of the competing technologies.[23] But without such laborious and sophisticated analyses, countervailing subsidies are likely to be inaccurate.

IV.
REVAMPING UTILITY DECISION-MAKING

The electric utility industry, which provides more than a third of this country's energy, is the United States' largest market for renewable technologies. As such, it plays a major role in determining renewables' future. Over the last 20 years, the industry has become somewhat more receptive to renewables, mainly because of new state and federal laws and regulations. But fossil fuels still provide the vast bulk of electrical services in the United States. As a result, the electric utility industry is responsible for about 68 percent of national SO_2 emissions, 36 percent of NO_x emissions, and 33 percent of CO_2 emissions. Shifting the nation's generation mix to renewables—in part to reduce these emissions—will require further reforms in utility regulation.[24]

Major Federal and State Initiatives in Electricity-supply Regulation

The utility market for renewable energy other than hydropower was initially stimulated by the passage of the Public Utilities Regulatory Policies Act (P.L. 96-917 or PURPA) in 1978. This law required utilities to purchase energy produced by qualifying renewable or cogenerating power facilities at "nondiscriminatory" rates. To become eligible for payments as "qualifying facilities" (QFs), renewable energy producers must fulfill federal requirements related to size, energy source, ownership, and other factors. Constitutional challenges were not resolved until 1983, but afterward the law's implementation progressed rapidly in some states. In 1989, Congress temporarily raised the maximum allowed PURPA-mandated power plant capacity from 30 MWe to 80 MWe (Sklar, 1990).

Most of the renewable electric capacity developed since the 1970s has had Qualifying Facility status. Roughly 17,000 MWe qualified under PURPA between 1980 and 1989, including 7,618 MWe of biofuels, 2,460 MWe of geothermal energy, 3,578 MWe of small hydro, 790 MWe of solar, and 2,226 MWe of wind power (Sissine, 1992). As shown in Figure IV-1, the number of new QF applications peaked in the mid-1980s. Whether the energy sources and technologies eligible under PURPA will continue to be the dominant source of new renewable capacity depends partly on other legal changes. In particular, 1992 federal energy legislation aimed at increasing competition in power generation gave renewable and nonrenewable independent power producers better access to utility-owned transmission capacity and also created a class of independent power producers exempt from the Public Utility Holding Company Act.

Over the same period that PURPA has been implemented, other utility resource planning and acquisition processes at the state level have been overhauled, partly in response to consumer and environmental concerns. Chief among these reforms is the notion of least-cost planning—a comprehensive planning process that considers the broadest possible range of demand- and supply-side resource options and results in the selection of a mixture of resources that meets customer demands for energy service at the lowest long-term social cost.[25] As of 1991, thirty-one states required some form of least-cost planning (Lamarre, 1991). These rules vary considerably, however, in the extent to which utilities are required to consider demand-side along with supply-side resources' benefits and costs to both society and ratepayers. In fact, most least-cost planning does not expressly consider avoided environmental impacts, reduced risks, and distribution, transmission, and reliability benefits, even though these benefits can exceed savings from avoided capacity additions and energy. Nor do the least-cost planning requirements in the 1992 federal Energy Policy Act explicitly address these issues.

Only a few states have resource acquisition regulations that recognize renewables' particular strengths and weaknesses. Partly as a result, ten states account for 73 percent of the national renewable QF capacity.[26] During the period that most of their renewable

Figure IV-1: Renewable Generation PURPA Applications

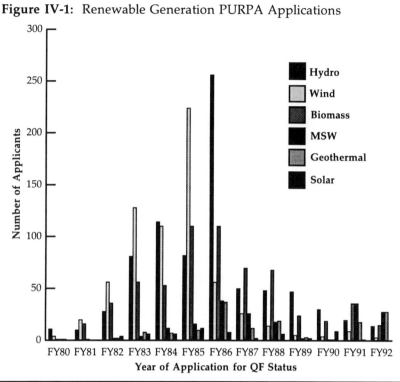

Source: FERC, 1992

capacity was being acquired, these states' regulatory provisions included standard, long-term contracts specifying predictable payments for both the capacity and energy value of the resource (Hamrin and Rader, 1993).

Not all state-initiated reforms have helped renewables command greater market share. Legitimate concern about cost effectiveness in the PURPA-enhanced electricity-generation market of the 1980s prompted some states to initiate bidding, in which renewable and nonrenewable generators sometimes compete to sell power to utilities. By 1991, some 36 states had some form of competitive bidding and 83 "Requests for Proposals" covering 21,141

MW had been issued. Competitive bidding emphasizes the cost of energy, which, in turn, is influenced by capital costs, projected fuel-prices, and discount rates, but not necessarily by characteristics that favor renewables.

Under competitive bidding, PURPA's "must buy" and "avoided cost" (defined below) provisions don't apply to renewables. Although 40 percent of all capacity acquired under PURPA has been renewable, only 17 percent of that acquired under bidding has, and two thirds of that consisted of projects based on woody biomass or geothermal energy (Hamrin and Rader, 1993). Even in the Pacific Northwest, where renewable energy flows are ample and environmental consciousness is high, total renewable capacity proposed in competitive bidding solicitations to date is insignificant compared to fossil-fuel capacity (Bain, 1992b).

Renewables in Today's Utility Environment

Despite past reforms, many utilities still lack the analytical tools and financial incentives needed to evaluate renewable options fairly. One key concept is "avoided cost"—initially defined under PURPA as the cost a utility would have incurred to purchase power from another source or to construct and maintain its own generation source if a QF had not supplied the power (AWEA, 1992). States determine avoided cost procedures and monitor the buy-back rate subsequently calculated by utilities, but the calculation methods vary widely. *(See Box IV-1.)*

As conventionally defined, avoided cost tends to be underestimated, so any ranking of resource options is biased against renewables. When calculations of avoided cost focus solely on the next power plant, key factors are neglected: variation in the cost of providing electrical services according to geographic location within the utility system or differences in time of day, fossil fuel-storage costs, and alternative ways of making electric service reliable. In addition, avoided costs are by definition strongly influenced by how much the "avoided fuel" is projected to cost. Avoided costs based on point estimates of future natural gas prices ignore the difficulty of predicting these prices as the range of natural gas uses increases over time—to wit, spot prices for natural gas varied by over 150 percent in 1992.

Box IV-1. Calculating Avoided Costs

The techniques used to estimate avoided costs were initially developed for making power purchases from nonutility sources. Two approaches for estimating avoided costs can be distinguished: direct measurement and application of tariff-like unitized values. Of the two, direct measurement more accurately estimates the avoided costs associated with generating capacity, energy, and transmission and distribution facilities. Direct measurement is sensitive to short versus long-run perspectives and the time and location in which load is avoided. Direct measurement of avoided costs also takes account of the scale of the resource to be acquired. Considered one at a time, renewable resource applications may avoid only short-run marginal (fuel and variable O&M) costs. But considered in the aggregate, they may defer or obviate the need for a future generating unit.

Under the second method, the estimation of unitized values, avoided costs are measured by multiplying the change in area under the load curve by the resource's unit value. Using tariff-like values is inaccurate to the extent that the actual load impact of nonutility generation differs from the assumed loads used to calculate avoided cost (Krause and Eto, 1988).

The direct measurement approach is analytically superior since it explicitly compares scale effects and other system costs incurred with and without resource acquisition. Thus, it can better capture the full value of renewable energy applications. The drawback is that it requires more information than the alternative method.

To take advantage of cost-effective opportunities to buy renewably generated power, build renewable energy generation, adapt electric or thermal end-use applications of renewables as demand-side measures, strategically locate distributed renewable power installations, or provide installations of renewables at remote sites, utilities and regulators must first understand how the characteristics of a particular resource affect its value. Few have all the information needed to do so.

PURPA induced utilities to collect enough data to defend estimates of avoided cost, but did not create economic incentives for them to find renewable applications in their service areas. As a result, data on the correlation of renewable energy flows with daily and seasonal load curves, requirements for integrating intermittent sources of energy to maintain system reliability, the compatibility of electricity from renewables with that of central-station power, and the integration of demand-side management with renewable resource flows are often unavailable.

Utility regulators also lack up-to-date data on renewables, so it's hard for them to develop a regulatory framework for identifying renewable applications, let alone promote utility decision-making processes that are fair to all competing energy sources. Compared to their knowledge of the technical, economic, and legal aspects of utility demand-management programs, PUCs know little about renewable energy. According to a 1990 nationwide PUC survey, 33 to 61 percent of the commissioners had no opinion about the efficacy of various regulatory policy options toward dispersed PV systems. Less than half of those surveyed had an opinion about future prospects for photovoltaics. In sharp contrast, 90 percent of these same commissioners were well-informed about whether their states' regulatory policies encourage demand-side management (Byrne et al., 1992b).

Perceived risks and utilities' lack of familiarity with renewables have meant that most renewable power has been developed by independent developers who sell power to utilities. True, PURPA opened up this market. But had they been more directly involved, utilities would now be more familiar with renewables and, presumably, less anxious about investing. Because renewable capacity is most likely to be independently developed, how utilities decide to acquire new power supplies has an effect on renewable power development disproportionate to that on non-renewable development.

Today, a utility's decision about whether to build or buy new capacity is affected by several factors, including some unrelated to the positive or negative characteristics of power-generation options. These include how power generation is deregulated, what competitive bidding and related requirements must be met in planning and acquiring capacity, how regulators allocate various financial risks and returns between utilities and independent power producers, and how a utility's appeal to its investors is affected by the proportion of purchased relative to utility-owned capacity.

Not surprisingly, utilities and regulators often overlook the potential cost advantages of building renewable capacity instead of purchasing equivalent power (Lamarre, 1992)—among them, the avoided expenses of negotiating power purchases and meeting PURPA requirements related to fuel, type, project size, and ownership. Compared to independent developers, most utilities have access to lower-cost capital, more land, and a broader range of options for integrating intermittent renewables with existing power sources.

Assessing Renewables' Strengths and Weaknesses

Utilities and policy-makers must come to grips with four common characteristics of renewables, which may have both positive and negative sides. First, most renewable energy technologies are modular, so their minimum cost-effective size is relatively small. Second, renewable generation facilities are expensive to build, though not to operate. Third, some renewable projects produce power intermittently—only when the sun shines, the rain falls, or the wind blows. And, fourth, renewable power projects must be sited where high-quality resources are found.

Some of the comparative benefits of renewables become clear only if utility executives and regulators explicitly consider uncertainty about future supply and demand in utility decisions. All else equal, an electrical supply portfolio that performs well under a range of assumptions about the future is certainly preferable to one that performs optimally under just one scenario (Meade and Teitelbaum, 1989). But although flexibility and freedom from dependence on purchased fuels reduce certain financial risks that can, in theory, be evaluated (Hirst, 1992b), widely accepted tools for doing so do not yet exist (Cadogan et al., 1992). Basically, utilities will have limited incentives to improve their risk analysis—and thus give renewables their due—until regulators change the way risks are allocated among stockholders, ratepayers, and independent power producers.

In general, the regulatory reforms discussed below call for changing either utilities' resource planning and acquisition practices (by, for instance, requiring the use of different analytical tools) or economic incentives (by, for instance, structuring rates to better reflect long-term location-specific marginal costs). If utilities operated in competitive markets, reconfiguring economic incentives alone might induce changes in how they plan and how they acquire capacity. However, the legal obligation to serve ratepayers at reasonable costs, combined with the high cost of getting and analyzing data, may keep PUCs from pushing hard for, say, marginal cost pricing in setting hook-up fees. In such cases, statutory changes are needed to resolve the trade-offs.

Modularity

Because most renewable energy technologies are modular, the capacity size at which cost is minimized is relatively small. This is reflected even in the average sizes of utility-owned capacity additions planned between 1991 and 2000 in the United States and Canada: oil and gas, 116 MW; coal, 315MW; nuclear, 773 MW; biomass plants, 26 MW; geothermal, 15 MW; hydro, 138 MW (NERC, 1991). The advantages of modular technologies—compared to those of conventional alternatives—are their short lead times (*See Table IV-1*), their ability to closely match load growth, and their potential to support a utility's transmission and distribution system.

Reducing Financial Risks and Costs. The cost of an incorrect electric demand forecast—whether excess capacity (resulting in capital payments for an underutilized plant) or a shortfall (necessitating bulk power purchases from outside the system)—can be substantial. Because future growth in energy demand will remain uncertain, technologies that allow a utility to add capacity incrementally as new information about changing load patterns comes in are increasingly attractive.

Since bigger units take more time to build, the probability of a mismatch between committed capacity (with its irreversible expenses) and forecasted energy demand is comparatively great with

Table IV-1. Lead Times and Unit Size Associated with
Different Types of Current Electrical Generation
Technologies[1]

Technology	Years[2]	MW
Gas Combustion Turbine (peaking)	2.5	75
Gas Combined Cycle	3	100–300
Coal-Fired AFB Combustion	7	500[3]
Nuclear Fission Reactor	14–15	1,000–1,300
Geothermal	<1–3	10–150
Hydroelectric	2–4	1–300
Biomass Direct Combustion	2–3	5-25
Utility Scale Wind	0–0.75	0.05–0.50
Solar Parabolic Troughs	1–1.5	30–80
Photovoltaic Modules	<1	<0.01

Notes:
1. Data based on 1991 CEC Energy Technology Status Report.
2. Generally from site selection to commercial operation.
3. Recent trends in advanced modular designs for coal-fixed
   generating stations (Dowlatabadi and Toman, 1991) suggest
   that their optimal size is 150–250 MW with correspondingly
   shorter lead times than that shown.

large plants. Projects with longer lead times are also more likely to
run afoul of changes in environmental and electricity-pricing regulation (Meade and Teitelbaum, 1989).[27] With modular energy technologies, in contrast, capacity can be added incrementally and
changes in the scale or location of the project can be made with comparative ease if load patterns change.[28] As long as generating characteristics are similar, employing modular resources to expand utility capacity affords investors the freedom to wait to invest instead of
committing capital to generating options with longer lead times.
This freedom is worth a lot: according to one empirical study, the

premium associated with delaying investment may be large enough to alter supply choices (Crousillant and Martzoukous, 1991).

The use of modular technologies can also reduce certain risks from unexpected disruptions of electrical supply services. For example, the probability of total power loss with 1,000 MW of modular electric capacity dispersed throughout a utility service area is less than that with a single 1,000-MW central-station facility. All else equal, maintaining electric service reliability in the system costs less when adding modular capacity than when acquiring large central-station capacity.

The use of so-called "distributed" applications can also cut transmission, distribution, and other costs (Rastler, 1992). Transmission and distribution costs already represent about half of all investment costs for many utilities, and this share is rising. In 1990 alone, investor-owned utilities spent over $9 billion on routine substation upgrading and associated utility investment (Moskovitz, 1992).

In an often-cited study, Pacific Gas and Electric (PG&E) modeled the costs avoided by installing a dispersed PV system as an alternative to investing in a new transformer and other related substation and distribution upgrades (Shugar, 1991). The case study found that PVs could relieve thermal overload on distribution system components, such as transformers; reduce line losses; defer transmission and distribution capacity additions for five to ten years; and reduce the costs of maintaining system reliability. Strikingly, the study also revealed that benefits other than capacity savings and fuel savings accounted for over half of the total estimated benefits to the utility system (Shugar, 1991). In any case, it's clear that renewable resources can in some cases be matched to local loads and used to relieve local distribution facilities for less than it costs to upgrade and maintain them.

Whether grid-connected or independent, modular renewables can also be used in homes or businesses to avoid costs for the utility. Under a Southern California Edison/Texas Instruments joint venture, rooftop grid-connected PV systems would eventually be installed on some homes of the utility's 3.6 million customers. More generally, PVs, solar domestic water heaters, and other end-use applications are cost-effective demand-side management options in some locations (Byrne et al., 1992b; Maycock, 1992; Stein, 1992), though few utilities finance them as alternatives to building new centralized power-generation capacity. With independent applications, a customer's energy requirements and distance from the grid determine whether a stand-alone or grid-connected electricity source is more cost effective. In many situations, employing stand-alone renewables is already less expensive than extending distribution lines because of savings in the repair, replacement, or upgrading of existing lines to small, remote, or otherwise hard-to-serve customers.

Most utilities ignore the impacts of a customer's location on the cost of providing service. When the United States was first electrified, private utilities competed against municipal utilities and independent power producers for the same customers, and area pricing (based on the recognition that the cost of providing electric service can vary widely within the grid) was a common practice. But this practice has fallen into disuse, and utilities have since been structured around central-station generating units that increased in size to achieve economies of scale. For this reason, the structure and cost of the transmission and distribution system has been determined by power generation. Indeed, even as planning for new generating capacity begins to shift away from maximizing plant size, large generating units with transmission lines emanating from them to serve local distribution systems are still at the center of the physical structure and mindset of virtually all utilities.

Realizing the Benefits of Modularity. To realize the economic advantages of switching to modular capacity, utilities and regulators must develop the analytical capability needed to estimate the effects of dispersed generation projects on transmission and distribution system costs, reliability costs, and line losses. In calculations of avoided cost, for example, potential savings from remote off-grid renewable applications must be compared to the costs of line extensions and service drop-off. All utilities should be required to compare costs for new hook-ups that require grid extensions with those of independent renewables, as some already do. In Colorado, the PUC now requires utilities to present potential customers with a cost comparison of stand-alone photovoltaic systems and conventional line extensions. Going one step further, a new electric rate class allows the Idaho Power Company to begin offering PV-based electric service to remote customers.

85

Since a primary purpose of least-cost planning is to better match supply to demand, all cost-effective resource flows and applications should be identified as long as the cost of doing so is low. Yet, data collection and analysis costs per unit of energy potentially supplied tend to increase as the size of individual renewable applications decreases. At some point, the value of improved decisions to the utility is canceled out by these costs. New analytical tools may be needed to cut the cost of evaluating small-scale applications of renewables (Shugar et al., 1993). (Evaluating distributed applications site by site as in the PG&E study is an expensive proposition.) For starters, industry should make screening tools more broadly available and the federal government should provide technical assistance to regulators and utilities to meet new planning demands.

To complement these planning changes, reforms in utility and customer incentives are needed. Hook-up fees should better reflect the full generation, transmission, and distribution costs of serving new customers, and current line-extension pricing policies that discourage utilities or customers from taking advantage of cheaper renewable applications should be reformed. Some utilities charge new customers only the "average embedded value" of all customer hook-ups. Others provide a distribution line of a certain length at no cost and charge the customer only for additional extension costs. (In Colorado, the Western Area Power Administration and a rural cooperative are jointly experimenting with the use of PVs for powering livestock-watering pumps—normally quite expensive to serve because they are small, far from electric lines, and subject to high weather-related maintenance costs (SERI, 1991). Ranchers have little incentive to participate, however, because the utility subsidizes the cost of line maintenance.) Cost-based incentives should be put to the test. If the total costs of extending and maintaining service conventionally were included in customer rates, stand-alone renewable systems that provide equivalent service would enter the competition on a more even footing.

Biases in Resource Acquisition. Developers of small renewable projects who want to sell power to utilities get a raw deal because contracting procedures are geared toward large projects, and the power sales contract that defines the economic, legal, and opera-

86

tional relationship between the utility and the renewable facility can be expensive to negotiate. Standard contracts would give regulators and all other interested parties a convenient and low-cost vehicle for considering a wide variety of price and non-price issues. The use of such contracts could help non-utility power generators reduce contracting costs and project lead times, especially for renewables with installed capacities of 10 MW or less. Currently, sixteen states require standard contracts for small QFs and only eight require standard contracts for QFs of any size.

Cost Structure

Since renewable energy technologies generally have high capital costs and low fuel costs, the financial requirements and risks associated with using renewable energy differ from those of conventional supply alternatives. To do justice to these differences, both analytical changes and reforms in utility planning and purchasing procedures are needed.

Risk Reduction. Adding renewable generation to an existing system can lower the financial risks of dependence on fossil fuels. Even if long-term fuel contracts (for which utilities pay a premium) have been signed or the utility owns fossil fuel resources, such unpredictable domestic or international events as labor disputes and regulatory changes can all raise fuel costs. Energy-transportation infrastructure—railways, ports, and pipelines—is also subject to acts of god. Independent of this infrastructure, renewable power generation is thus immune to such risks.

Adding renewables to a mix of power-generation sources dominated by coal, gas, or oil can smooth out utility cash outflows. In contrast to those associated with oil and gas, the operating expenses with renewables are relatively fixed. Moreover, oil and gas prices tend to correlate positively with periods of high demand—a definite drawback for investors seeking stable revenue requirements.

Normally, returns from more risky investments require higher discount rates. Most utility analyses, however, typically compare different resource options using the same discount rate (normally, the utility's weighted average after-tax cost of capital), and the utility's overall cost of capital reflects the average risk from its investments. But applying an aggregate discount rate gives higher-yielding but potentially riskier investments an edge over technologies with high capital costs but low financial risks (Awerbuch, 1993).

One approach to considering the relative risks of resource options is to require utility planners to use different discount rates for certain projects or individual technologies (Awerbuch, 1992; Meade and Teitelbaum, 1989). When projects' revenue requirements are discounted at the correct risk-adjusted rate, competing projects can be ranked accurately. In one case study, risk-adjusted discount rates were estimated for coal-fired steam at 6.5 percent, combined cycle-gas turbine at 4.5 percent, and photovoltaics at 11.5 percent, which made PVs look more attractive (technically, their present worth revenue requirements were lower) than the gas turbine option—the frontrunner if the same discount rate was used in all three energy options (Awerbuch, 1993). In general, discount rates should be differentiated in evaluating both utility-built and purchased power projects since society faces the same fuel-cost risks in either case.

Since risk-adjusted discount rates are common in other industries, why don't utilities use them? Historically, one power-generation option was roughly as risky as another, so using single discount rates probably make sense. Just as important, regulators have allowed utilities to shift some risks away from shareholders to customers, so utilities have had little incentive to use more than one discount rate. Forty-two states allow utilities to pass on fossil-fuel price increases to ratepayers, and most such fuel-adjustment clauses also apply to the energy portion of purchased power costs. Small wonder that fuel price stability has not been a primary concern in choosing generating technology (Palmer et al., 1992).

Risk adjustment in utility planning won't be effective unless it is complemented by attempts to shift an appropriate share of the risks to shareholders. One wise move might be for PUCs to limit automatic fuel-adjustment pass-throughs. While ratepayers can respond to price signals by using energy efficiently, utility managers are in a better position to choose long-term generation supplies.

Reforming Contract Terms. Renewables' cost structure deters investors in other ways too. Contract price terms between independent power producers and utilities determine the timing and pattern of utility payments (as distinguished from overall price levels). They can profoundly influence which technologies are economically viable. If energy and capacity payments aren't timed to meet the needs of renewable power developers, the technology probably won't be deployed. Currently, only ten states have contract provisions and payment schedules even nominally consistent with renewables' cost structures (Hamrin and Rader, 1993).

Because independent renewable energy projects are capital intensive and outside investors often insist upon relatively short debt-repayment periods to reduce their risk, a developer's cash outflows in early years could exceed payments based on avoided costs. To get around this problem, some power-supply contracts allow payments that exceed avoided costs in the early years of the agreement and lower payments in later years. Under such "front-end loaded" contracts, payments decline over the contract period, so their net present value remains equal to that of payments under more conventional agreements. More capital-intensive technologies (such as PV, wind, and solar thermal) would require higher initial payments than those with relatively low capital but higher operating costs (such as biomass).

On balance, front-end-loaded cost recovery—not entirely new to the utility industry—better meets renewable power producers' financial needs and enhances their competitiveness. Not all PUCs allow such contracts, however. More frequently, their use is discouraged through negative weighting factors in bidding or the addition of financial security requirements to contract provisions. A key concern is that front-end loading leaves ratepayers vulnerable. Who pays for replacing capacity, for instance, if a project fails in its later years? Fortunately, this concern can be addressed without discouraging the development of renewable resources. The key is structuring the flow of energy-related payments so that they exceed the variable operating costs of production and allow a reasonable margin to cover unforeseen expenses throughout the project's life. Under this principle, it will always be in a developer's financial interest to continue to keep a plant open. Indeed, even if the initial developer goes bankrupt, another will find it advantageous to operate the facility. Of course, requiring energy payments to exceed predicted O&M costs and building in some margin for unpredicted costs will limit the amount of front loading possible.

A related issue is contract duration. When an electric utility constructs a power plant, regulation creates an implicit contract between the utility and ratepayers over the useful life of the plant, typically 30 to 40 years. If it is well-managed and extraordinary circumstances don't intervene, the electric utility is allowed to recover the capital and operating costs of the plant over its entire life, regardless of future fluctuations in fuel prices. A regulatory contract that limited utility cost recovery to 10 or 15 years would put an end to virtually all construction of utility power plants. Yet, for renewables, some states arbitrarily limit contract terms to, say, 10 or 15 years, all but blocking development. Only four states require utilities to make long-term (15- or 30-year) contracts available, and only 13 specify that standard offer rates must include significant payments for providing generating capacity (Varanini, 1992). Fixed, predictable payments for energy and capacity would provide Qualified Facility developers with the long-term price certainty needed to obtain financing for long-term projects with high capital costs. At the same time, contract reopeners or suspension clauses, which also make financing difficult, should be avoided.

Intermittency and Lack of Dispatchability

Renewable resources that provide power only when the wind blows, the sun shines, or the rain falls are often assumed to have no capacity value as additions to the utility's generating system. Typically, utility-owned conventional power plants are considered dispatchable (that is, kWh output can be varied daily or hourly to follow changing system loads) while PV systems (whose power output varies according to sunlight intensity) are not.

Many PUCS and utilities overemphasize the problems associated with intermittent power sources, especially since these sources will constitute only a small share of a system's power supply for the near future. In some states, non-utility generators can't get long-term contracts unless power output can be controlled to meet utility demand. In others, dispatchability is a requirement for capacity-related payments. Still other states treat dispatchability as a primary non-price weighting factor when resource options are ranked. When utilities contract with intermittent QFs under

PURPA, they typically specify power-reliability requirements.[29] While dispatchability is certainly desirable, utilities that make it the crux of decisions about adding capacity will dismiss intermittent renewables out of hand. But the issue is more complex. The predictability and dispatchability of renewable and non-renewable generation varies widely by technology. No power plant has a capacity factor[30] of 100 percent: some scheduled outages are unavoidable, and unpredictable circumstances affect fuel availability and plant operation. Even baseload fossil fuel and nuclear plants operate only 70 to 80 percent of the time.

If reason prevailed, dispatchability and intermittency would be considered nothing more than price factors to be incorporated into calculations of avoided cost. For example, wind generation is not dispatchable, but the coincidence of high wind and peak load may make a wind project as desirable as a dispatchable resource. Seasonally, wind resources are very predictable, allowing maintenance to be scheduled during low-output periods. Similarly, though PV systems are not dispatchable, their operating and reliability characteristics in relation to local or system-wide daily load patterns (especially air conditioning) in many cases make these systems as valuable as dispatchable resources of equivalent size.[31] A utility can accommodate short-term variations in power by exploiting its system's ability to absorb some fluctuation in current. According to a case study of PG&E, reliability wouldn't decrease at all, even if 35 percent of system capacity were derived from intermittent renewables without storage, as long as the operation of dispatchable units was adjusted optimally (Johanssen et al., 1992).[32] Each utility's ability to accommodate intermittents is different. Adding 1,400 MW of wind capacity to Northern States Power Company's system would slightly increase reliability over a fossil-fuel based capacity-expansion plan, though costs would rise by 2 percent (Brower et al., 1993).

Borrowing techniques used to analyze Demand Side Management (DSM) resources (which may also be variable), regulators and utilities should determine how adding an intermittent resource affects the operation of an entire system. One option is looking to so-called hourly dispatch models, which find ways to minimize the cost of meeting electric load as it changes throughout the day.

Besides correcting misperceptions and improving analytical techniques, utilities should look for ways to increase the value of intermittent renewables to their systems. Some utility systems have plants scheduled for retirement or industrial customers with on-site generation facilities; both should be evaluated to see if they can provide back-up capacity to meet peak demand. In some situations, it may even be cost-effective for the utility to add low capital-cost back-up capacity to increase a project's dispatchability and, thus, its value.

By exploiting diverse resource flows in their service areas, utilities can smooth out their natural weather-related output. Under this "portfolio" approach, the total power output of intermittent renewables has more capacity value than the sum of that of individual projects. For example, the combined hourly output of two wind turbines distant from each other might be more stable than that of two turbines on the same wind farm. Similarly, two resources—say, solar and wind—might be matched with each other to have more combined capacity than they would if each were developed alone.

In the long run, if intermittent capacity came to represent a sufficiently high percentage of a utility's total capacity, it may be necessary to add supply-storage—for example, modular pumped hydro—so that intermittent renewables could operate much as dispatchable energy sources do. Demand-side storage is an option too. As one example, where the availability of windpower predictably lags behind or leads system peaks, thermal storage could be added at the point of end use (Chupka and Howarth, 1992). Because energy losses during storage reduce net energy production, however, the extra costs associated with these losses must figure into any evaluation of this approach.

By changing how other generating units are dispatched, exploiting regional portfolio effects, or pursuing other options that entail some cost, most utility systems should be able to integrate significant amounts of intermittent capacity cost-effectively. Unless they are constructing intermittent capacity themselves, however, utilities currently have little incentive to identify technical options that enhance the value of intermittent resources to their systems. The alternative is for independent renewable generators to firm up

92

capacity themselves. Bundling projects in a range of locations to sell power to one or more utilities is one option. Another is using renewables in renewable/fossil hybrids or with fossil or other back-up capacity located elsewhere. Such options would allow renewable developers to compete with nonrenewable power producers for utility solicitations limited to dispatchable power (Hamrin, 1992b). Yet, because renewable developers can't take advantage of the system-wide opportunities that would be available to the purchasing utility, their options are likely to be relatively expensive. Besides prohibiting dispatchability requirements, regulators should thus require utility planners to fully evaluate least-cost measures for integrating intermittent renewables.

Alternative Approaches to Influencing Utility Decisions

Many of the regulatory reforms discussed so far to change utility resource decisions require utility planners or regulators to quantify the resource-specific characteristics of generating options under an Integrated Resource Planning (IRP) framework. But since quantification can be difficult and expensive, some PUCs now require utilities to qualitatively weigh the nonprice attributes of resource options (such as fuel diversity) considered important in the utility service area. When such attributes are considered in competitive bidding, renewables are more likely to be selected (Swezey, 1992).

The obvious disadvantage of a qualitative approach is that it substitutes value judgments for more objective estimates, sidestepping the valuation problem rather than solving it. Consequently, some regulators are considering other ways to change utility supply choices, approaches that do not require planners to place quantitative or qualitative values on individual resource characteristics. One option is to regulate the quantity of renewables acquired.

Under this "dedicated acquisitions" approach, utilities would solicit bids only from resources with certain desirable characteristics, such as low environmental impact. One version is the "Green RFP"—a competitive request for new capacity limited to renewable resource projects. The scope of this type of Request for Proposal resembles that of existing utility RFPs for demand-side resources. A Green RFP combines the cost-control aspects of competitive bidding with an RFP's ability to reduce market risks to renewable resource developers. This new tool lets renewable resource developers know that factors other than price per kWh are important and spares them the high transaction costs and other problems encountered in open-ended, all-source bid solicitations (that may involve such competitors as gas turbines).

At present, New England Power has issued a (45-MW) Green RFP, Bonneville Power Administration has received bids under a solicitation for 50-MW of wind capacity, and Portland General Electric has announced it will issue a 200-MW Green RFP. The Sacramento Municipal Utility District recently recommended a 350-MW set-aside for renewables and other advanced generation technologies (Swezey and Sinclair, 1992). At least two states have also ordered utilities to acquire specified amounts of renewable capacity: New York (300-MW) and California (300-MW).

Whether competitive or not, dedicated acquisitions have advantages and disadvantages compared to reforms of planning processes. Dedicated acquisitions can take into account a whole set of attributes without time-consuming and contentious economic analysis. Set-asides let developers know the quantity of renewables that regulators consider it prudent to acquire within some price range. True, the process for determining the size of set-asides is not totally objective, but then neither are regulators' attempts to incorporate the nonprice characteristics of renewables.

A peril of using some combination of approaches to incorporate renewables' values is double-counting. Regulators must, for example, avoid simultaneously quantifying nonprice attributes in resource planning requirements while establishing set-asides based on the same set of resource characteristics.

Siting Characteristics[33]

Developers of solar, wind, hydro, geothermal, or biomass resources can locate energy-production facilities only where the cost of producing energy is competitive with existing power options. While insolation changes gradually by region, wind energy can vary greatly within a mile. Hydrothermal facilities can be built only over certain geologic formations. Hydroelectric sites require drops in river elevation. Biomass isn't economical unless it is already being collected for another purpose (such as lumber or pulp processing) or can be grown within 50 miles or so of where it is to be converted to power.

Of course, fossil fuels must be transported too—whether by rail, barge, or pipeline facilities. But whereas a renewable generation project's size may be constrained by local resource availability, conventional fossil fuel capacity is often large enough to justify construction of dedicated facilities if none already exist.

Other factors further constrain the range of acceptable sites for renewable energy facilities. Access to transmission capacity poses greater obstacles for renewables than for fossil-fuel projects.[34] An independent renewable project may not be able to compete with nonrenewable power projects for limited existing transmission capacity if its capacity is less, its "power quality" incompatible with that needed for grid stability, or its capacity factor relatively low. At the same time, adding or upgrading transmission capacity to accommodate renewables may be prohibitively expensive. In the case of solar and wind resources (intermittent sources with relatively low capacity factors), acquiring firm transmission capacity is more expensive per unit of energy transmitted than for conventional non-peaking plants. While proximity to transmission capacity is critical, developers must also be able to acquire resource rights at reasonable cost and be accepted by local residents.

Incidence of Social Costs

Concentrated where energy is produced, the social costs of renewable energy are distributed quite differently from those of conventional energy sources. A wind farm's effects are immediate, visible, and local. (See Table IV-2.) In contrast, the impacts of fossil fuel production are far flung: extraction, transportation, and conversion of energy resources to electricity typically occur in different locations, and air pollution may cross state and even national borders. For example, while the area required per kWh for producing coal-fired electricity is similar to that of several renewable technologies, almost 90 percent of the land required for coal's fuel cycle is for mining.

Table IV-2. Relative Severity of Potential Impacts from Different Renewable Electricity Facilities[1]

	Land Requirements	Water Pollution	Air Pollution
Solar Thermal Electric	+		
Photovoltaics	+		
Wind	+		
Dedicated Biomass	++	++	++
Municipal Solid Waste			++
Geothermal Heat		+	++
Hydroelectricity	+	++	

+ = Moderate impact relative to other renewables.
++ = Severe impact relative to other renewables.
Note:
1. Based on OECD, 1988.

Despite renewables' comparative "cleanliness," public opposition to new renewable projects can be adamant. Almost axiomatically, it is easier to politically mobilize a relatively small number of individuals with much at stake than a large number of those with little to gain or lose (Olson, 1965). In the case of a proposed wind project, the many individuals benefitting from reduced reliance on fossil fuels are less likely to take a stand than the handful of property owners fearing drops in land values. A wind project may thus face opposition disproportionate to its size and the social costs associated with its fuel cycle.

This problem reflects the locus of public decision-making. Broad energy planning and policy choices tend to be made at the state, regional, or federal level, while most land-use decisions are made locally. Institutional mechanisms for balancing the net social benefits of using various energy supply options with their distrib-

Solid Waste	Noise	Visual Intrusion	Ecosystem
		+	+
		+	
	+	++	+
++		+	++
++	+	+	
	+	+	+
		+	++

utional effects don't exist, and current energy regulatory processes are too fragmented to do the job. For example, when federal hydro-power facilities are relicensed, the environmental impacts of the project under consideration are reviewed, but not the impacts of alternative generating options.

Except for hydro and MSW facilities, siting has usually not been a deal-stopping problem for renewable energy facilities. But most experience has been limited to one decade and to certain regions. Because the growth and diversity of renewable energy development have been greatest in California, the kinds of siting conflicts encountered there may recur as renewables become a significant part of the energy mix in other regions. *(See Box IV-2.)*

Siting is especially controversial if renewable projects are proposed for previously undisturbed land. As pristine places grow scarcer, the recreational, aesthetic, and so-called existence values

Box IV-2. California's Siting Experience

Initially, policy and market factors in California helped make the environment for renewable energy development more favorable than it is likely to be again anytime soon in California or anywhere else. In the late 1970s, California's population and electrical demand were growing rapidly, and the state was unduly dependent on oil-fired generation. At the same time, the public had a relatively high level of environmental consciousness. Other factors also came into play. Public policy gave energy supply diversification, based partly on renewables, a high priority. Buyback rates under PURPA in the 1980s were based on natural gas prices high enough to allow developers to comply with site-permit requirements (such as habitat replacement by solar electric developers for the desert tortoise and Mojave ground squirrel) without jeopardizing the project's financial health.

With avoided costs (based on gas prices) now lower, the profit margin of renewable energy developments—and, hence, their ability to absorb siting-related costs—will fall. In some cases, site-mitigation requirements may reduce renewables' environmental cost advantage over that of competing nonrenewable energy technologies (Varanini, 1992).

While the near-term market and policy environment for renewables may not be as favorable as it was during the early 1980s, land development regulation in California appears as strong as ever. And because California utilities are not seeking to add large central-station generating facilities and are fulfilling part of their projected demand growth with Demand Side Management (DSM) programs, even small supply-side additions tend to be subjected to greater scrutiny than they were during the early 1970s.

placed on undisturbed areas are rising and environmental regulations are getting tougher. Birds-of-prey deaths associated with some wind farms in California have become a public issue, while the need to let salmon run on the Columbia River has limited total hydropower capacity in its watershed. Concern about ecological diversity could also translate into limits on intensive biomass production (Cook et al., 1991). Siting some fossil-fuel capacity may actually be easier if utility-owned units or industrial cogenerators can be shoehorned in at existing power-production or industrial sites (Kahn, 1992).

Population, urban, and economic growth will also increase the potential for conflicts among residential, agricultural, recreational, and energy-related uses of land. In one California county where a wind facility was proposed, the residents polled significantly preferred wind energy to fossil, nuclear, or biomass electric generation, and another survey found wind-facility development more popular with affected residents than housing development. Nonetheless, in at least two instances housing developers successfully blocked wind projects. Such conflicts can only intensify as both types of developers vie for affordable land in the future (Thayer and Hansen, 1991). Wind developers in the Midwest will have to negotiate with more landowners than early developers in California did because the midwestern tracts of land tend to be smaller and many more support crops (Lamarre, 1992).

Increased land-use conflicts and the resulting increases in siting-related costs per unit of capacity for all energy sources are likely to work against renewables. Also, because energy demand is growing only modestly, all new energy-supply projects are coming under greater scrutiny than they once did (Varanini, 1992). And because renewable projects are novel, energy developers may have to wait for local policy-makers to promulgate siting regulations (Bain, 1992a). Such delays might raise the cost of capital while design changes for environmental reasons, legal expenses, and the denial of permits can sap project momentum.

Legal gaps and red tape in siting could reduce some of the comparative advantages renewables now enjoy. For instance, the advantages that renewables have had over fossil and nuclear plants in construction lead time would be reduced if the waiting period for approval of siting small energy facilities increases. One goal of policy reforms should thus be to reduce siting lead times while effectively involving the public in siting decisions.

99

Mitigating Siting Impacts

A key lesson from California's experience is that renewable energy developers must take environmental concerns seriously. Public concern over siting impacts simply can't be dismissed as an example of the "Not In My Backyard" (NIMBY) syndrome. Public acceptability of future projects may well depend on how well visual and other impacts are minimized, and on the project's efficient operation (Thayer and Hansen, 1991).

Where resource flows are adequate, developers should use already disturbed sites—such as abandoned military bases—and lands already used for compatible purposes. A major PV installation in the Swiss Alps minimizes aesthetic impacts by mounting modules along existing transportation right-of-ways (Nordmann et al., 1991). As for development on other land, zoning laws could help energy projects avoid competition with residential or other land uses. For example, minimum distances separating these facilities from other types of development might be established in land-use plans. According to a statewide survey of California, the percentage of residents who approve of a wind facility increases with its distance from their homes (Thayer and Hansen, 1991).

Better Balancing Benefits and Costs in Siting

Most current institutional processes for resolving land-use disputes are expensive. Public opposition to facility siting can lead to litigation, and few friendlier or cheaper models for coming to terms exist. At the same time, public trust that government institutions will not approve undesirable land uses is low (Peelle, 1988). What's more, the public prefers resource policy options that involve no social risk, and in the case of electricity production, the existence of excess capacity and the mistaken perception that near-term energy needs can be met solely through increased efficiency feed this desire.

Mediation, consensus-building, citizen juries, and collaborative policy forums are all alternatives to legal confrontation. An early example using mediation was when hydropower development was proposed in New England under PURPA—most notably, at Swan Lake in Maine (Talbot, 1983). While residents didn't completely overcome their distrust of the developer through this

100

process, the development was modified before it was built. In general, the success of mediation depends on the skills of the mediator and the sense among all parties to the dispute that participating in mediation is in their self-interest (Talbot, 1983).

An alternative to mediation is consensus-building—a technique recently used in a geothermal development in the scenic Newberry Volcano area in central Oregon. By 1987, more than 30 wells had been drilled on the volcano and more than 200,000 acres leased for geothermal development. Of these, 13,000 were within the boundary of the proposed Newberry National Monument. A local consensus was reached among 30 interest groups through a long series of meetings. Like mediation, consensus-building works to the extent that stakeholders perceive a self-interest in participating in a time-consuming process, that negotiating proceeds on the basis of "interest" and not "positions," and that all parties support the outcome (Collins, 1990).

Along with alternative forms of dispute resolution, more"proactive" regulatory reforms should also be considered. If regional or even state-wide generic siting proceedings for renewable energy resources were established, prime sites for developing renewables could be identified. Energy developers who later apply to use these sites could then be reasonably sure that they are complying with state environmental laws. Also, such preliminary proceedings might help balance local and state siting concerns during the final hearings. Testing this idea, the Northwest Power Planning Council has a new program to assess energy resources, identify mitigation measures, develop and test procedures for siting and licensing facilities, and devise demonstration projects (Hamrin, 1992a). To reduce the siting risks facing developers, states should provide information on regulatory processes to them as early as possible in project development (Bain, 1992a).

Finally, utilities should consider economic mechanisms that help distribute social benefits and costs equitably. Communities are certainly more likely to welcome siting facilities if they expect to gain (OECD, 1988). Indeed, the high success rate for siting biomass plants in California has been attributed to the perception of local economic benefits (Eaton, 1991). One option is direct compensation. Nearby communities could be given a break on power rates or a guarantee of rate stability in return for hosting a wind farm or other renewable generation facility. Alternatively, developers could set aside land for community parks, as some have already done.

The near-term procurement pressures (low avoided costs and strong competition) facing independent power developers provide an incentive to not fully incorporate environmental-mitigation expenditures into their bid prices. But if potential siting-related costs are left out when bids are submitted, winning bidders may find revenue streams too low to meet them (the so-called "winner's curse"). If renewable capacity is acquired noncompetitively, independent power developers may also face low avoided costs if near-term projected natural gas prices are low. Under both forms of procurement, the need to make a profit limits how much environmental compensation developers can provide (Varanini, 1992). (In contrast, utilities can often recover unforeseen environmental mitigation costs from ratepayers.)

The most important mechanism for addressing conflicting incentives in competitive bidding is to require that all likely social costs of all the resource options be as fully reflected in bid prices as is practical. To capture site-related costs, PUCs should work with state environmental agencies to ensure that any environmental-mitigation and related downstream costs are consistently incorporated into all bids (including any submitted by the utility).

Improving Transmission Access

Power can't be sent to the utility in which the renewable resource is located or to another utility with higher avoided costs unless access to transmission capacity is adequate. In some cases, expanding the geographic area over which renewable power resources can be tapped to supply utility needs would make intermittent renewables more cost effective. For example, peak power output from an intermittent resource may coincide better with the system peak of a utility in a different time zone than with one closer. Such sales are attractive if the gain in avoided cost exceeds the "wheeling" costs of moving power.

The 1992 federal energy legislation strengthens FERC's authority to require private utilities to provide transmission access to independent developers. But physical access does not necessarily ensure fair prices, especially when transmission capacity is constrained; and regulators have yet to resolve important cost-allocation and other issues. Moreover, even under the new law, FERC is required only to respond to requests for transmission access, not to require integrated resource planning in conjunction with its regulation of electric utility holding companies, wholesale power purchases, or transmission capacity sales.

Transmitting renewably generated power to load centers entails a real cost that must be considered when alternative energy-resource acquisitions are compared. Nonetheless, federal and state regulators can ensure that different generating options receive equal access to transmission services. First, FERC should issue rules that minimize the procedural costs and fairly allocate the capital costs of necessary transmission upgrades between utilities and developers. Even with mandatory transmission access, the costs of petitioning FERC and negotiating with a utility may be prohibitive for small developers. Second, FERC should also take more initiative in transmission planning. It might, for instance, convene and fund forums where it could meet with regional blocks of states to consider transmission needs. Alternatively, FERC could authorize regional planning by blocks of states, allowing them to formulate joint long-range plans that take transmission capacity into account. Authority for insuring that renewable resources are considered at the regional level falls between the traditional regulatory purviews of FERC and the states, so legislation may be needed. Precedent for regional planning exists in the federal mandate for the Northwest Power Planning Council. In addition, FERC should analyze the U.S. transmission system comprehensively to identify where upgrades or construction are needed to open access to major renewable resource areas in the United States, especially where transmission bottlenecks are already a problem.

Since many transmission transactions are local, states should issue regulations that insure continued intrastate transmission access and fairly allocate costs between utilities and renewable developers. This move is especially important where competitive bidding is required. If utilities, regulators, and developers have equal access to information on line losses and the costs of providing transmission services, all parties can evaluate the full costs of a bid (including transmission services) relative to other projects. In California, the PUC is already developing transmission cost tables for three major utilities. In Ohio, the PUC has proposed under its competitive bidding program that winning bidders should be able to wheel power to the receiving utility if they are not in its jurisdiction. Under the Ohio proposal, utilities must themselves coordinate any necessary transmission system additions and upgrades (O'Driscoll, 1992).

V.

CHANGING ENERGY USERS' INVESTMENT INCENTIVES

Another major market for renewable energy technologies besides supplying electric power is in reducing purchased energy needs in homes and businesses. These so-called "demand-side" technologies include solar water heating, passive and active solar space heating and cooling, wood heating, "ground-source" heat pumps, daylighting, and solar heating for industrial processes. PVs have also been attracting interest for demand-side applications. If electricity is included, residential and commercial buildings account for over a third of total U.S. energy consumption, so the potential of demand-side applications is enormous. Moreover, the thermodynamic quality and small scale of renewable technologies is well matched to a range of energy uses, accounting for much of the initial interest in solar energy. Insolation, for example, can be efficiently converted to provide space heating and cooling, which comprised 77 percent of total residential energy consumption in 1990. *(See Figure V-1.)* These same two end-uses comprised an estimated 68 percent of commercial-sector energy consumption, and furthermore, lighting accounted for another 17 percent (EIA, 1993),—an indication of significant electricity-saving potential through daylighting. Industrial process heating, which could be provided by solar applications in much of the country accounts for 12 percent of U.S. primary energy consumed (Mueller, 1990).[35]

Despite an initial burst of public and private-sector activity in the 1970s, demand-side applications of renewables have not come close to achieving their potential, either in absolute terms or relative to the market penetration achieved in some other countries (say, Japan and Israel, where solar hot water systems are widely used). When the impetus for consumers to reduce purchased

Figure V-1: Residential Energy Use
Major Categories, 1990

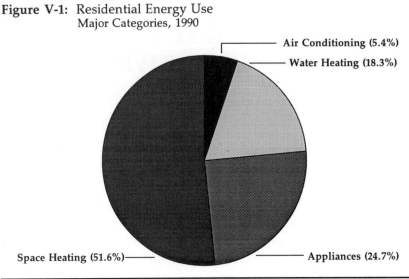

Air Conditioning (5.4%)

Water Heating (18.3%)

Space Heating (51.6%)

Appliances (24.7%)

Source: Thompson, 1993

energy costs waned in the 1980s, renewable energy applications, perceived to be less cost effective than efficiency measures, were hit especially hard. The way most buildings, developments, and communities are now designed commits occupants to energy consumption levels based on expectations of continued low energy prices. Unfortunately, retrofitting these buildings later will invariably be more costly than designing and constructing them with long-run social costs of energy in mind. Solar access and street orientation, solar water heating, and ground-source heat pumps are all more cost effective in new construction than retrofits.

The obstacles that demand-side applications of renewables face often resemble those facing major energy-efficiency investments. Various barriers create private disincentives to invest in renewable energy and efficiency measures that (from society's perspective) cost-effectively reduce fuel consumption:

    1) price signals that do not reflect the long-run incremental costs that energy use imposes on electric and gas utilities;

2) high investment risks due to sunk costs combined with uncertainty over lifetime cost savings in purchased energy;[36]
3) high information costs incurred in researching one-time energy-investment decisions; and
4) differences among the goals of those making energy decisions—for instance, those who make building design decisions and those who pay the resulting energy bills.

These barriers are, in turn, exacerbated by others. Often, energy-saving retrofits compete with non-energy building investments. Further, the conservative building industry faces competitive pressure to minimize construction costs (Vine and Harris, 1988; Carlsmith et al., 1990; Sioshansi, 1991).

Experience has shown that these barriers can be scaled by policy tools, such as information services, financial incentives, and regulations. Most of what has been learned from past policies to reduce building energy consumption through energy efficiency improvements can also be applied to renewables. While many energy-efficiency measures are very inexpensive, the relative importance of renewables in reducing building energy needs is likely to grow as efficiency measures saturate their markets and the cost of saving energy by using renewables comes down. Achieving the potential energy contribution from demand-side renewables will require not so much developing new policy tools as applying existing ones to renewables.

The recommendations put forth in this chapter are aimed at improving policy tools so that the potential contribution of renewables to building energy needs can be achieved. Programs for encouraging energy efficiency measures have been implemented since the early 1980s, but debate persists over whether they have been a good use of society's resources. From society's perspective, program cost-effectiveness is determined not simply by comparing actual energy savings to the capital and labor costs of installing equipment. The costs of administering the program and its attribution rate (the proportion of total installations that would not have occurred without the policy tool) must also be considered. Policy tools should, of course, encourage installation of only those energy-saving measures that are cost-effective in their own right. But cost-effectiveness can be further improved by choosing policy

107

tools with expected high attribution rates, organizations that can minimize program costs, and implementation methods that sustain high rates of participation.[37]

Choosing the Right Tools to Promote Renewable Energy Investments

Reforming energy price signals to the extent practical should be the first step in improving energy users' incentives to make energy-saving investments because doing so may obviate the need for more expensive policy initiatives. But step two is coming up with other policy tools for overcoming the remaining critical barriers to specific investments in energy efficiency or renewable energy.

Improving Energy Price Signals

Even if environmental costs were fully internalized and government subsidies to mature energy technologies ended (as proposed in Chapter III) energy price signals would still be biased against renewables. Utility regulators commonly base electric and gas rates on a private utility's average rolled-in costs rather than on the full marginal cost of providing energy services. For example, new gas customers rarely face the full cost of acquiring new natural gas supplies, though these costs are projected to rise, and new electricity customers are rarely charged the true cost of extending power lines to them. Some customers served by public utilities enjoy subsidized electric rates as well. In contrast, a renewable or energy efficiency investment is typically priced by vendors at its full marginal cost.

From society's perspective, investments in renewables or energy efficiency might be viewed as attractive even when they are not appealing to individuals. Natural gas rates that reflect current supply-replacement costs may not be enough to prompt changes in building design and construction.[38] So, before potentially expensive new policy initiatives are implemented, energy price signals need to be reformed to more accurately reflect the relative social costs of alternative energy choices.

In particular, regulators should require utilities to reform rate structures to prompt customers to fairly consider renewable and efficiency options. The reforms should be in the direction of marginal cost pricing. Time-of-use rates, for example, would fully credit reductions in electric load during periods of peak demand. Similarly, if rates were differentiated by zone, demand-side resources at locations in the grid where service costs are high would be more fully valued. And if hook-up charges better reflected the need to add generating and transmission capacity that new customers impose on the grid, the building industry would have an incentive to construct more energy-efficient buildings.

Improving Investment Incentives

Even if price signals were improved, energy consumers and the building industry might not respond. Investment returns are subject to uncertainties related to future energy use in the building; future prices of displaced purchased energy; the lifetime performance of equipment; the quantity of renewable energy flows; the duration of building ownership; and investors' ability to recoup their investment through an increase in the building's resale value.[39] In addition, renewable energy equipment sized and designed for a specific building, and often integrated into the structure itself, may have a low salvage value. Not only is the would-be investor committed to an irreversible investment (Hassett and Metcalf, 1993), the longer an investor waits to obtain the information needed to reduce uncertainty, the greater the foregone returns.

For new construction, builders are often unsure whether improvements that reduce energy requirements and (for passive solar) improve building comfort and aesthetics will attract buyers or tenants. A 25-percent reduction in energy costs may yield only a 2-percent reduction in total rent per square foot—probably not enough to sway a renter one way or the other (OTA, 1992). New home buyers may not be willing to pay extra for energy features, and optional energy upgrades may give the impression that the base home is not energy efficient. In addition, construction techniques new to a builder also involve risk of cost overruns. For these reasons, builders require high rates of return on renewable energy features (OTA, 1992).

Since energy users decide whether to make other investments on the basis of their risks and returns, why should the government intervene to make energy-saving investments more attractive? One reason is that capital markets don't allocate energy investments on the basis of their risks and returns to society. Investments in new energy infrastructure and in reducing energy demand both help meet society's future energy needs. But individual energy users, who typically pay more for capital than do utilities that make supply-side investments and may have to stay put for a long time to profitably amortize energy-saving equipment, can't be condemned for taking a more parochial view.

Investments in measures that lower energy purchases would be more attractive if lenders recognized that, by reducing cash outflows, such investments are safer than many other building improvements. Consider energy-efficient mortgages (EEMs), which are based on the principle that reducing monthly energy bills through energy efficiency or renewable energy investments increases the amount of household or business income available to meet mortgage payments. If lenders were to offer EEMs, the mortgagee's risk of default would presumably be less than if the mortgagee had invested in other improvements. While EEMs have been available for several years and are being tried out in a federal pilot program, they should be promoted more aggressively and be made available for commercial buildings. So far, lenders remain to be convinced that default risks are lower with buildings that have low energy requirements, and secondary mortgage institutions have to date been reluctant to tell primary lenders what types of loans to make. Because the secondary mortgage companies have not promoted EEMs, lenders have not marketed them to realty agents and builders who, in turn, do not understand that EEMs can qualify buyers for bigger loans. Accordingly, only 0.03 percent of home mortgages have been EEMs since they were first made available.

More costly approaches to making the cost of capital commensurate with the risks of renewable and energy-efficiency investments have also been tried—below-market loans, grants, rebates, and tax incentives. The Solar Energy and Energy Conservation Bank, created by the Energy Security Act of 1980, exemplifies one approach. The bank was to have made $525 million available during 1981 through 1983. But the funding was cut 95 percent under the Reagan Administration, and states used 80 percent of the remaining funds for conservation measures instead of renewables (Sawyer, 1986). Not until 1992, when federal housing legislation authorized a similar institution, the Solar Assistance Financing Entity, was the concept of a renewable energy bank resurrected. State loan programs for renewables were common in the early to mid-1980s. As of 1991, eighteen states still had some form of loan program for alternative energy investments, though some restrict loans to conservation and energy-efficiency measures and target only certain groups. In Texas, for example, only state agencies, local governments, and school districts are eligible (Interstate Solar Coordination Council, 1991). For their part, at least twenty-two utilities now offer rebates, grants, or loans to customers investing in renewable energy equipment, and several others are planning such programs (Shirley and Sholar, 1993; Tempchin, 1993).

Tax credits, exemptions, and deductions constitute yet another type of financial incentive to increase the attractiveness of investing in renewable energy equipment. Federal tax credits for solar energy equipment were available to homeowners from 1976 until 1985, and state tax incentives were also common during that time. Approximately 26 states still offer some type of tax incentive (NATAS, 1992).

A problem common to tax incentives, loans, and similar financial incentives is that, while attractive to participants, they are expensive per installation that can be attributed to them. The sparse data available suggest that the proportion of individuals receiving the incentive who would not have otherwise made the investment without it, is low. An analysis of the federal residential energy tax credit found that a 10-percent increase in the value of the credit resulted in only a 0.5-percent increase in the probability of a conservation investment (Hassett and Metcalf, 1992). Another study found that past tax incentives were somewhat more effective in stimulating investment in solar heating devices than in less costly efficiency measures, but still had a small effect. Not surprisingly, fossil-fuel savings per dollar of foregone tax revenue turned out to be higher for tax credits for energy efficiency than for solar equipment (Sawyer and Lancaster, 1985). These and related findings suggest that such incentives be implemented only after less costly approaches have been exhausted.[40]

Increasing Information

While some energy investment risks (such as from fuel price uncertainty) can be offset by making investments more attractive, often more and better information can reduce other risks. Even by the mid-1980s, consumers weren't familiar enough with renewable energy applications to adopt them widely (Farhar-Pilgrim and Unseld, 1985). Despite almost two decades of accumulated commercial experience, a lack of accurate information still inhibits the market penetration of end-use applications of renewable energy. Moreover, renewables must overcome negative reputations since some early applications were expensive, inefficient, physically unattractive, or ineffective. On balance, such nonfinancial factors as system reliability, warranty protection, and confidence in suppliers may be as important as initial system costs in the investment decision. Thus, information on proper design to capture renewable energy flows, long-term performance, back-up or storage requirements, etc., is needed to reduce uncertainty about anticipated returns.

Homeowners and homebuilders also share misperceptions about the upfront costs of passive solar buildings. The major extra investment is not for additional equipment, but rather for additional design fees. One analysis of a subdivision showed that the proportion of attached single-family housing with solar access could be increased from 42 to 80 percent without changing density, amenities, or circulation patterns. For multifamily housing, the proportion of units with solar access could be increased from 38 to 90 percent, with only a small increase in density and concomitant decrease in costs (Tucker and Tumidaj, 1991). Clearly, far too few developers understand the opportunities for improving solar access.

Finally, popular understanding of how renewable energy and energy-efficiency measures can complement each other in attempts to minimize a building's overall purchased-energy requirements is poor. Making a structure's space-conditioning equipment and appliances more energy efficient might reduce energy requirements to levels that renewable energy applications with thermal and electric storage could meet (Parody, 1992). Where energy costs are high, it may even be cost-effective to design new residences to provide all their own energy.

112

Why do information gaps persist in various segments of the building industry? For starters, builders have little economic incentive to acquire the information needed to change construction practices. The problem is especially acute with small builders, who base construction techniques on past experience (OTA, 1992). Even large builders and their architects may not know much about energy-efficient design and construction techniques. (Prescriptive building codes create an incentive to learn only the least expensive way of complying with code requirements, not to go beyond.) Appraisers too need retraining: even though current FHA rules allow home buyers to roll the cost of solar hot-water retrofits into their FHA-backed mortgages, appraisers remain uncertain about the effect of the retrofit on a house's appraised value, making it hard for owners to capture the full resale value of the retrofit.

Various public and private organizations have operated public information services, training and education programs, energy audit programs, and product performance services. As discussed below, some of these programs have been more effective in improving knowledge of renewable energy applications than others.

Information and Training Services. Federal renewable information programs have tended to favor homeowners over businesses and industry, even though the residential sector uses less than half as much energy (Sawyer, 1986). Current federal energy-information programs—including those of the Conservation and Renewable Energy Inquiry and Referral Service, National Appropriate Technology Assistance Service, and National Renewable Energy Laboratory—serve diverse information needs. But many building-industry professionals don't realize that they can get "state-of-the-art" information materials from these programs (Vories and Notari, 1991).

Several states also offer information programs for homeowners and businesses. The Florida Solar Energy Center (FSEC) responds to inquiries and publishes a variety of materials for the general public. Hawaiians get free advice about residential renewable energy use through state-sponsored spots on radio and television and print media advertising. Florida, North Carolina, and other states have walk-in or call-in information services.

Other information programs are oriented more toward professionals in energy-related fields. The Passive Solar Industries

Council holds workshops on passive design and construction techniques and distributes guidelines for building-industry professionals. The Arizona Energy Office provides technical assistance for building photovoltaic-powered homes. Texas recently opened a solar energy center for building professionals. The FSEC conducts training programs for utility employees, construction contractors, architects and engineers, and planners (Florida Solar Energy Center, 1990). The city of San José conducted a training program for developers that addressed the mistaken notion that orienting developments to capture solar energy is more expensive than conventional development, the unavailability of simple measures to determine solar potential, and the lack of awareness of renewables' benefits (Tucker and Tumidaj, 1991). And national appraisal standards have been developed for the retrofit and new home markets for solar hot-water systems.

How well various combinations of renewable energy and energy-efficiency features perform depends on how they fit with the rest of the building. For this reason, improving understanding of a building's overall energy performance may be as important as garnering additional information about whether individual pieces of equipment or building components perform as expected. Building professionals and trades people need to master the concept of whole-building energy performance, and the associated measurement techniques should be stressed in training programs.

Energy Audits. Energy audits have been used to provide information on renewables to potential users. Under the National Energy Conservation Policy Act (NECPA) of 1978, Congress established the Residential Conservation Service (RCS) to provide home energy audits for single-family homes and separately metered all units in multifamily dwellings. States carried out the program through utilities, which performed the audits and sometimes provided further assistance, including information about suppliers and installers of recommended measures and help arranging financing. A federally authorized commercial building audit program was never implemented. Although the RCS law has expired, several states still require utility-sponsored audits.

Utility auditors may make general recommendations to customers about the potential for renewable energy applications. In practice, though, most auditors do not quantify their analysis of renewable energy retrofit potential, much less evaluate cost-effectiveness. Although utility customers claim to value these audits, they probably don't stimulate renewable energy investments by themselves; at best, they encourage recipients to seek out more specific information. Energy audits for homes and businesses should thus be combined with other programs to increase the likelihood that recipients will make cost-effective investments.

Equipment Performance Data. Some early solar equipment performed poorly, and a negative legacy remains. Moreover, the lack of standardized performance and cost-saving data can limit buyers' ability to compare the cost-effectiveness of competing fossil-fuel-based and renewable energy equipment, thus increasing perceived investment risk. Such perceived risks can be reduced by programs for testing, certification, warranty, and standard setting for renewable energy equipment.

Certification of solar collectors by the Solar Rating and Certification Corporation or the Florida Solar Energy Center is mandatory under a number of state incentive programs, and standards for photovoltaics will soon follow (Solar Industry Journal, 1992). But more is needed: certification should be required for *all* renewable energy equipment commercially marketed to end users. Currently, only eleven states require or recommend certification of solar energy equipment under these programs, and though certification is in most cases an eligibility requirement for receiving state solar tax credits or for other state programs, noncertified systems can still be sold (Interstate Solar Coordination Council, 1991). Seventeen states require solar contractors to be licensed (Solar Industry Journal, 1993); others should follow suit.

Overcoming Institutional Barriers

Even if information, investment incentives, and price signals are improved, institutional constraints sometimes prevent the implementation of energy efficiency or renewable energy measures with short payback periods (often the case with passive solar design). In particular, the parties responsible for paying fuel bills commonly do not have the authority or the incentive to make capital investments. Incentives may be split between tenants and landlords, builders and home buyers, and even among divisions within corporations and government agencies.

The choice of policy tools depends in part on whether the investment decision is for new or existing buildings. For new construction, a regulatory approach may be necessary to reduce the energy requirements (to levels justified by cost-effectiveness) of segments of the building market that are not amenable to other approaches. But if regulatory approaches are not the first line of defense, they can nevertheless be improved. First, since many local laws and regulations have not kept pace with improvements in building design and construction techniques that minimize energy consumption, they should be revised. If building codes were based more on energy performance, they would give builders greater flexibility in choosing the most appropriate techniques for a particular site and also promote technical innovation. If they were developed on the basis of whole-building analysis, then energy-efficiency, renewable energy, and even storage measures could better complement each other. And if regional or national codes and standards were implemented at the local level for the fragmented building industry, the energy efficiency of the nation's building stock could be improved more quickly.

Second, other regulations governing land use should be reviewed to ensure compatibility with attempts to maximize solar gain. Laws governing solar easements, solar provisions in zoning and land-use planning, and "minimum solar access" requirements should all be scrutinized (Johnson, 1979). In addition, local solar rights laws should prohibit homeowner associations from restricting the use of solar energy.

For the retrofit market, other policy tools are needed to scale institutional roadblocks. Large public and private organizations may have incentives to purchase the energy equipment that has the lowest levelized life-cycle costs of different options. A survey of purchasers conducted for the city of Seattle found that, among the procurement criteria considered, maintenance ranked highest, followed by compatibility with existing equipment, availability, quality, and first cost. Energy efficiency and lifecycle cost were ranked below all five (City of Seattle, 1988). Part of the problem is that few municipalities even have accounting systems set up to monitor the energy consumption of different departments. In most communities, the past spending patterns of departments largely determine next year's budget, and target funding for the department is often reduced to the level actually spent. In Houston, for example, budgets are reviewed without considering energy-management efforts. Other budgeting requirements also intrude: in Houston, energy management is inhibited by a twelve-month limit on most expenditures (City of Houston, 1989).

To make energy-equipment decisions in large organizations more consistent with efforts to minimize lifecycle costs, the incentives of budget and procurement officers need to be changed. For example, municipal budget directors should consider instituting shared savings, segregated energy funds, or energy savings payback funds. Similar tools are needed for other levels of government[41] and private corporations.

Improving Policy Implementation

Policies already in force would be more cost-effective if they were seen as parts of a coordinated strategy for changing how energy-users make decisions. Building regulations improve the energy performance of the least efficient building stock, but do little to shift the industry as a whole. Local officials may not have the training to implement model energy codes or the incentive to aggressively enforce them. Information programs reduce uncertainty about how an added energy improvement should perform, but, by themselves, may not reduce other financial risks. And financial incentives—whether in the form of tax breaks, low interest loans or otherwise—will have little impact on investment rates unless geared to overcoming risks as perceived by target audiences. In the building industry, the competitive pressure to minimize first costs in new construction may overwhelm financial incentives intended to induce energy-saving investments.

Integrating Policy Approaches

Individual programs need to be linked to a long-term strategy for reducing energy consumption in new and existing construction. Opportunities for combining policy approaches should be exploited to reach all relevant decision-makers, cover the entire range of building stock (from low-end to leading-edge builders), and address the multiple barriers to renewable energy investments. Because regulations give builders no incentive to exceed minimum energy standards, they would more effectively reduce new building energy requirements if paired with economic incentives.

Under a feebate system used by the Sacramento Municipal Utility District (SMUD) for new construction, Sacramento's developers pay the full cost of extending utility service to new developments less a rebate that reflects the extent to which the new buildings exceed energy standards. While neither the technical challenges of incorporating passive solar design into such systems nor the administrative problems involved are trivial (Wirtshafter and Hildebrandt, 1992), connection feebates for new construction merit wider use.

Greater use should also be made of combined education and regulatory approaches to promote passive solar design. Since providing solar access for a significant proportion of units in a new subdivision need not cost more than conventional design (Tucker and Tumidaj, 1991), local subdivision ordinances should require minimum solar access, and training programs for developers should familiarize participants with these ordinances. The Bonneville Power Administration has combined financial incentives and builder education to support upgraded energy-efficiency provisions in the region's building codes (Vine and Harris, 1988).

An example of coordinating information programs with targeted economic incentives is using building energy-rating systems in combination with energy-efficient mortgages (discussed earlier), as ten states are doing or considering (Solar Industry Journal, 1992). If point-of-sale energy disclosure and economic incentives are combined, they are much more likely to influence energy-purchase decisions. SMUD's solar hot-water program combines quality assurance (through system certification, quality control, and training) with performance-based customer rebates (Murley et al., 1993).

Developing Marketing Strategies

Programs designed to spur investment in renewable energy applications would be more effective if designed and implemented in the context of an overall marketing strategy (Katzev and Johnson, 1987). Marketing strategies and technical support services can increase both program participation and energy savings (Vine and Crawley, 1991).

Marketing strategies should include an analysis of more than the financial factors affecting decisions to adopt an energy measure. If energy choice were based solely on money, how information is presented would be less important. But motivations are not merely economic, especially for homeowners. According to a national survey, solar buyers also take environmental protection, personal satisfaction, and self-reliance into account (Farhar-Pilgrim and Unseld, 1985). Recognizing these motives would help architects and engineers market energy-design techniques to builders. In turn, given homebuyers' concerns, builders should make passive solar energy features a more visible selling point.

Information services should reflect how people perceive and use information. Such variables as the type of information, form of presentation, type of media channel, and message credibility and saliency all come into play (Dennis et al., 1990), as does the timing of information releases. Endorsements by opinion leaders can lend credibility to an innovation, and information programs tailored to smaller, more homogeneous subsets of program participants may be more effective than broader appeals. Also, new information channels may have to be tried to reach the new construction and retrofit markets, as well as such professional groups as tract-home builders and architects.

One useful way of presenting potential buyers with information on a building's level of energy efficiency is through a rating system. While a few states and utilities are developing home energy-rating systems, the energy contribution of renewable applications—such as passive solar design—is rarely well incorporated. Builders and sellers should be required to disclose "whole building" energy ratings, including renewable energy features, at the point of sale.

Federal economic and technical assistance may be needed to encourage state and local implementation of national programs, such as model building codes and home-energy rating systems. High front-end costs, such as those incurred in retraining local officials and informing consumers and the building industry of new programs, may be too much for some states to bear alone.

119

Evaluating Cost Effectiveness

The cost-effectiveness of most of the disparate public and private programs for reducing energy consumption in buildings has never been properly evaluated. This makes it hard to know the optimal size of financial incentives or strictness of building codes. Indeed, most such programs lack evaluation requirements, which makes it hard for managers to choose among program alternatives and improve program cost-effectiveness.

Much remains to be learned about what works and why. For example, while financial incentives generally spur greater energy savings per participant than information programs do, they are not necessarily more cost-effective (Hirst et al., 1983). The cost-effectiveness of loan programs depends on loan-processing and other administrative costs, default rates, and, most important, the extent to which loans lead to the installation of equipment that would otherwise not have been considered. And because of continuing concerns over the rate impacts of demand-side management (DSM) programs, promotion of renewable energy measures by electric or gas utilities is likely to be limited until questions concerning the cost-effectiveness of such programs are answered.

To overcome these hurdles, systematic performance monitoring and evaluation should be required of all government and utility programs aimed at reducing energy consumption (whether through efficiency improvements or renewable energy applications). Estimates of cost effectiveness should ideally be based on measured energy savings induced by the program. Program budgets should thus include adequate funding for monitoring and evaluation.

Choosing Appropriate Institutions to Promote Demand-Side Applications

In some cases, tools to stimulate investment in renewables are best implemented by utilities. In others, government-sponsored programs are needed. Which institution should conduct the program depends on what barrier is being addressed, who benefits versus who bears the costs, and what organization can minimize administrative costs. For example, utilities already have regular

120

contact with electric and gas users; their credibility can be used to help deliver demand-side program services. But some local communities or energy service companies may be able to deliver DSM programs more cost effectively than utility staff.

Traditionally, utilities resisted encouraging any measures that reduced electricity sales because their profits were tied to such sales. One of the most significant reforms in utility regulation in the past ten years has thus been for states to place demand- and supply-side resources on a more equal footing as they create financial incentives for utilities. Thirty-two states have in place or in progress mechanisms that allow a utility to recover revenues lost to DSM measures or to share the economic benefits of efficiency improvements with their customers. As of 1991, state regulatory policies toward DSM ranged from account-balancing procedures for reconciling actual DSM expenditures with amounts budgeted and recovered (11 states), rate-basing of DSM expenditures (19 states), lost revenue recovery (13 states), and demand-side mechanisms that, for instance, allow the utility to receive higher returns on DSM expenditures (22 states) (Reid, 1992). Eighteen states had no regulatory provisions for encouraging DSM.

As regulators remove utilities' overall disincentives to invest in demand-side management measures, renewable energy applications can join energy-efficiency measures on the menu of options. While relatively few utilities have included renewable applications to date, technical improvements and cost reductions among several renewable applications (especially those that reduce both peak demand and energy use) merit their more frequent consideration. For example, passive solar designs can reduce peak space-heating loads, which are often costly for the utility to serve.[42] Similarly, utilities with significant electric water-heating loads should consider solar water heating as a DSM measure, as several are now doing. PVs are also cost-effective demand-side management options in some locations, though few utilities finance them as alternatives to building new centralized power-generation capacity (Byrne et al., 1992a; Maycock, 1992; Stein, 1992).

Utilities can play various roles in reducing risks facing potential renewable energy users. At one extreme, a utility could be the legal owner of the renewable energy system, bearing turnkey installation (minus a customer contribution), maintenance, and replacement costs and charging the customer normal rates for metered energy use. Alternatively, the utility could provide financing at its cost of capital and recover its investment through monthly utility bills. It could also provide product guarantees or monitor equipment performance. Finally, the utility might merely provide customers with an approved list of service providers: customers get maximum choice and receive cost savings, while the utility minimizes its own risk.

Electric utilities can justify spending ratepayers' money on programs to encourage builders and ratepayers to invest in renewable energy applications as long as benefits to ratepayers outweigh costs. The choice of which specific economic test to use is controversial because of the potential for nonparticipating customers to subsidize participants.[43] In any case, electric utility investment in renewable measures that substitute for non-electric uses cannot be justified on the basis of ratepayer benefits.

End uses served by renewables can also be served by natural gas, fuel oil, or propane. Especially when gas prices are expected to rise or gas peaking costs are high, gas utilities and their ratepayers may benefit from DSM programs. In fact, the 1992 Energy Policy Act mandates extending the integrated resource planning concept to gas utilities. *(See Chapter IV.)* Passive solar design can also be cost-effective as a gas utility DSM measure (Aitkin and Bony, 1993).

In cases where substantially greater benefits accrue to society as a whole than to ratepayers, it may be necessary to look beyond utilities to government agencies to deliver programs to reduce building energy requirements. Because its risks can be spread among many projects and shared among many taxpayers, the government's discount rate is typically lower than that of private utilities, giving it an advantage in offering financial incentives. Equity issues must still be addressed, however; past renewable energy tax incentives have been generally regressive, helping more affluent groups most (Dubin and Henson, 1988; Rich and Roessner, 1990). Choosing the most appropriate delivery institution thus requires carefully assessing program benefits and costs from different accounting perspectives.

VI.

ACCELERATING INVESTMENT IN RENEWABLE ENERGY COMMERCIALIZATION

Getting a technology to commercial maturity—the point at which it can provide energy services reliably at an acceptable price and suppliers can provide warranties, maintenance, and replacement parts—typically requires research, development, demonstrations, and market diffusion. Scientific research and technology development conducted in laboratories yield findings vital to decisions about whether to go forward with the commercialization process. Demonstrations, in turn, inform commercial designs, test the viability of the technology under real-world conditions, and reduce cost and performance uncertainties. Finally, suppliers must get products to consumers in the quantities demanded at competitive prices.

Throughout all these stages of commercialization, constant market feedback is needed. Successful product design entails innovations not only in the initial research stage, but often in manufacturing and marketing as well (Kline, 1990). On balance, commercialization is driven more by market feedback than by science.

No technology will reach commercial maturity, of course, unless the private sector decides to back it instead of alternative investments. Moving from R&D to full-scale demonstration typically requires a jump in the magnitude of investment. Scaling up production capacity to lower unit costs requires yet another such jump. To private investors, many emerging technologies simply don't seem worth the risk. Indeed, returns on investments in R&D pay off only if some commercial product results, and limits on how long individual firms can profit from information generated by R&D cut into any such pay-offs.

Why Government Should be Involved

Since many emerging technologies and industries that can't attract adequate private investment vie for public support, why does renewable energy commercialization deserve public support, especially during a period of fiscal constraints? The short answer is that the only way to capture the considerable social benefits of renewables is to speed their development. As explained in Chapter 2, some such benefits depend on how quickly renewables replace fossil fuels or are poised to do so. While some applications of renewable energy would penetrate markets sooner if the reforms in energy pricing recommended in Chapter 3 were set in motion, others would not. And not all the social benefits of using renewables can realistically be incorporated into energy prices. Nor will the redirected incentives recommended in Chapters 4 and 5 for utilities and energy users necessarily induce needed investments in commercialization.[44]

Both the structure of energy markets and the nature of renewable energy technologies make renewables a hard sell to private investors. As exemplified by the Luz bankruptcy, energy markets are seen as risky: extremely unpredictable, complex, heavily regulated at the federal and state levels, and subject to manipulation by oligopolists and foreign governments. Changes in federal and state tax policies, changes in energy R&D priorities over the past decade, and an evolving regulatory system for the sale of electricity to utilities only aggravate apparent risks (Fenn and Williams, 1991).

The cost of energy from several renewable energy technologies has substantially decreased since the early 1980s (Larson, Vignola, and West, 1992; Weinberg and Williams, 1990). A California utility implementing a solar water-heater incentive program watched costs fall by 30 percent in a single year (1992) and expects further decreases as the number of installations rises (Murley, Osborn, and Gorman, 1993). While industry projections may be too optimistic, trends strongly suggest that economies of scale, technical innovations, or advances on learning curves could bring down the costs of several renewable technologies.[45] *(See Figure I-1.)*

There are no guarantees that potential cost-reductions for renewables will be achieved. Continued reduction in the cost of renewable energy is partly a function of increased production, which requires investment capital. *(See Table VI-1.)* Yet, much of the renewable energy industry faces a "Catch 22": it can't achieve potential economies because it is undercapitalized, but can't attract enough capital because current demand isn't large enough to convince investors of the potential for cost reductions through increased output.

The high market-entry costs and rapid technological changes typical of many emerging industries also discourage private in-

Table VI-1. Required Annual Production Per Company to Achieve Potential Cost Reduction for Selected Technologies in California

Technology	Capacity Increment	Cost Reduction[1]
Wind	75 MW-100 MW	20%–60%, depending on technology
Hydrothermal	50 MW	10%–15%, site-specific
Solar Thermal/ Trough	80 MW-200MW	20%–40%, after regaining previous cost track
Photovoltaic	10 MW/ technology	50%–70%, depending on PV technology and on cost reductions in BOS
Biomass Integrated Gasification	200 MW	30%, relative to biomass steam turbine generation

Source: Aitkin, 1992, based on an industry survey.
Note:
1. Cost reduction projections are based on data provided by renewable energy equipment manufacturers.

vestment in the production of renewable energy equipment. These factors increase the possibility that a few firms will come to dominate the renewable equipment manufacturing industry, limiting healthy competition.[46] At present, for example, a single firm controls most wind-turbine production in the United States.

Given these factors, the rate of return to the nation as a whole from commercializing a renewable energy technology far exceeds what any single firm can capture. But the likelihood of social returns exceeding private returns does not, by itself, suggest how much and what kind of public support any given technology deserves. For that, other criteria must be applied.

One of two general approaches to bolstering private investment is for government to reduce private risk or to increase private returns through tax incentives, regulatory reforms (such as in antitrust regulations), trade policy, the protection of intellectual property rights, or other measures. Although some (notably, tax incentives) involve significant public outlays, others entail only modest administrative costs. The other general approach is government investment in R&D, demonstrations, or procurement. This form of support tends to require comparatively greater public outlays, since equipment must be purchased, and critics say that public funding displaces private investment and that government often backs the "wrong" technologies. On the other hand, it guides commercialization more directly—for example, through competitive multi-year procurements of specific technologies aimed at reducing unit costs. Both types of government support, of course, also result in some efficiency losses to the economy and transfer of investment away from other economic activities that must be balanced against the benefits of accelerated development.

Improving Public Investments

Most direct government investments in renewables have been aimed at the pre-deployment stages of commercialization. Indeed, the federal government has invested in research, development, and demonstrations (RD&D) in renewable energy since the 1970s, though it has spent far less on renewables than on several competing energy technologies. *(See Figure VI-1.)*

Figure VI-1: Energy R&D Spending
($billions, 1992 constant)

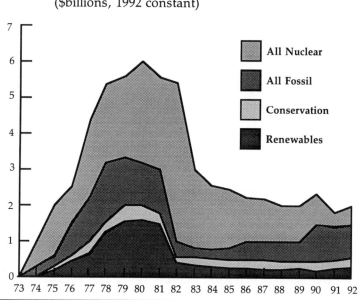

Source: Sissine, 1992

Before the first oil embargo, solar research had been linked primarily to the space program, and commercial applications received little attention (Sklar, 1990). The mid- to late-1970s saw the consolidation of energy research from several agencies into the new Department of Energy. Under the Carter Administration, energy research funding grew rapidly—to over $700 million in 1981. Early DOE funding was directed to large-scale, centralized projects, such as solar satellites, solar power towers, large-scale wind machines, and ocean-thermal energy-conversion plants. Cost-effectiveness was not an overriding concern. Even simple solar water heaters were designed with high solar conversion efficiency uppermost in mind, not cost-effectiveness (Sawyer, 1986).

During the 1980s, research and development funds declined precipitously. In FY90, the United States spent $84 million on renewable energy, down 90 percent in constant dollars from the FY79 peak (Sissine, 1992). Most remaining funds went to long-term re-

127

search and development, rather than to market-oriented commercialization activities (U.S. GAO, 1981).

The 1992 budget for renewables increased to $204 million, the first real increase in a decade. As shown in Table VI-2, photovoltaics commanded the biggest share, followed by biofuels, solar-thermal, geothermal, wind, ocean energy, solar building, and small hydropower. The FY92 renewables budget emphasizes investments with relatively short-term payoffs.

Several states have also invested in renewable energy RD&D. During the 1970s, states divided their budgets roughly equally among research, development, and demonstrations (Roessner, 1980). In recent years, some states have recognized that their comparative advantage lies in developing and transferring local applications of renewable energy technologies, not basic research. *(See Box VI-1.)*

Lessons from Past Public RD&D

The level, consistency, and management of RD&D activity have all been adversely affected by inattention to market diffusion. For most of its history, government energy spending has followed the "pipeline" model—a linear sequence of research, development, demonstration, and market-adoption activities. The premise has been that technologies can be pushed into the market without feedback along the way from would-be users. As a result, the selling points of some renewable energy technologies (such as their modularity) were often ignored. Under the pipeline model, wind and solar thermal-electric demonstrations approached prevailing fossil-fuel technologies in scale, but did not reliably produce energy. Even in cases where a technology passed field tests, provisions for getting it to market were seldom made (Kelly, 1992).

The level and timing of all energy investments has also been heavily influenced by political ideology and pork-barrel politics (Cohen and Noll, 1991). Various energy technologies have been held hostage to political ideology regardless of their merits, so overall investment priorities have been skewed as it changed with administrations (Frankel, 1986; Cohen and Noll, 1991).

In addition, the energy crises in the 1970s created strong competition for government funding that led lobbyists (both suppliers and other advocates) for all energy technologies to overstate na-

Table VI-2. FY92 Department of Energy (DOE) Renewable Energy R&D Funding

Program Area	($ Millions)
Solar Buildings	2.0
Photovoltaics	60.4
Solar Thermal	29.1
Biofuels	39.3
Wind	21.4
Ocean Energy	2.0
International	2.0
Technology	1.0
NREL	11.5
Resource Assessment	1.2
Program Direction	4.7
Program Support	0.9
Geothermal	27.2
Small Hydro	1.0
Renewables Total	**203.7**

Source: Sissine, 1992.

tional benefits. Feverish lobbying generated unrealistic cost expectations. In principle, energy research expenditures should be viewed as buying information to guide larger technology investments, but early budget allocations were overly focused on short-term expectations. When these weren't met, the new programs were cut before their full results were available to help those designing later programs (Cohen and Noll, 1991).

The tendency toward "pork barrel" spending on energy has also worked against the national good. Most energy funding has been allocated to serve local constituencies. Fusion and breeder reactor research facilities were big enough to find champions in Congress. On the other hand, support for photovoltaics (PVs), the highest funded renewable technology (Cohen and Noll, 1991), has not followed this pattern. More generally, support for all energy

---

Box VI-1. State RD&D Programs

While many states conduct some renewable energy RD&D, a few stand out. The Florida Solar Energy Center (FSEC) funds projects that demonstrate innovative applications of photovoltaics and solar technologies that have yet to become widely used in the state. With full-time staff of 85, including about 13 university faculty members, the FSEC has a wide variety of laboratory facilities, including a passive cooling laboratory, photovoltaic tracking stands, and computer facilities. In 1990, FSEC gave research grants totalling about $3,760,000, about 37 percent of which went to renewable energy projects (FSEC, 1990; Solar Industry Journal, 1992). The New York State Energy Research and Development Authority solicits research proposals to accelerate development of technologies and products that can use renewable energy sources to displace non-renewable sources. Areas of research run the gamut of renewable technologies and include electric and thermal load-leveling techniques and institutional factors in solar and wind turbine deployment. California is another state with a substantial renewable energy R&D program.

RD&D dwindled in the 1980s as memories of the energy crises faded, but renewable technologies were especially hard hit.[47] In contrast, the breeder program outlived its R&D rationale (Baily and Chakrabarti, 1985). DOE's energy technology priorities continue to be influenced by politics. *(See Box VI-2.)*

The up-and-down track record of renewable energy RD&D has contributed to investors' fears that renewables represent high risks. Several well-publicized early demonstrations were plagued by operational problems, and many technologies have not yet logged sufficient operating experience to dispel early concerns. While a small number of investment firms have now developed niches for financing renewables, most still lack up-to-date information (Fenn, 1989). To the extent that perceived risks are higher than actual risks, investment costs are inflated.

130

Box VI-2. DOE R&D Planning

When it made its 1991 budget, the U.S. Department of Energy assessed the potential of all major program areas to meet four national goals: enhancing national security by reducing oil import vulnerability, meeting future electrical demand, building up the national technological infrastructure, and promoting environmental quality. Energy technologies were also ranked by potential impact of increased government funding. According to the DOE official responsible for the exercise, which was used to set funding priorities, "[T]his package reflects the results of a considerable effort to develop, on its merits, program planning priorities in tune with the NES. Political sensitivities can be applied later..." (Stuntz, 1991). Although the outcome of this exercise supported increased funding priorities for conservation and renewables relative to fossil and nuclear technologies, the budget priorities DOE ultimately submitted to Congress were another story, indicating that political sensitivities favoring fossil and nuclear technologies were subsequently "applied" (Rezendes, 1992).

Improving Public Investment in RD&D

What are the elements of a cost-effective RD&D strategy for renewable energy? First, energy funding should be allocated to achieve national objectives based on the entire portfolio of investments. Second, RD&D investments should be integrated into a broader market-led commercialization process. Third, political influence in decisions about research and demonstration projects should be reduced. And fourth, private investors should be required to share risks.

Allocating Public Funding. During the 1970s, success was evaluated in terms of individual projects. But whether an individual project results in a technical innovation should not be the only yardstick. Rather, a portfolio of RD&D investments should be chosen to maximize the achievement of national objectives, even though the full commercialization of any individual technology may be uncertain. Thus, an energy portfolio consisting of many relatively small projects may be preferable to one of comparable cost based on a few large projects.

The portfolio approach also suggests a balance between short- and long-term projects. Not all worthwhile projects will have immediate pay-offs or even a high probability of success. Current federal RD&D for renewables emphasizes technologies nearing commercial maturity, stranding very uncertain but potentially high pay-off technologies (such as hot dry rock). De-emphasizing all long shots could kill important technologies, given venture capitalists' unwillingness to fund their development.[48]

Renewable energy technologies with a long-term potential to yield high payoffs belong in the federal RD&D portfolio. All else equal, the further a technology is from commercial maturity, the greater government's role should be. Conversely, the closer a technology is to commercial readiness, the more private sector support should be required. (Of course, public support must be allocated carefully to minimize the risk that public funding is merely displacing private investments.)

Finally, a portfolio approach to renewable RD&D policy calls for both basic and cross-cutting research projects (ORNL, 1989). The technical feasibility and market penetration of different technologies may be interdependent (Tolley et al., 1989), and some projects are complementary. For this reason, individual projects within a portfolio may affect each other's probability of reaching commercial maturity. For example, variable speed drive technology was developed to improve the performance of commercial motors and only later applied to wind turbine technology. And while much research has been conducted on building components, relatively little has been devoted to optimizing the design and construction of a building as an energy-using system. Then too, not all cross-cutting research is technology-oriented. For example, better understanding of risk perception is needed so that the public participation processes for siting renewables can be improved and regulatory costs kept consistent with project scale and impact. DOE's current organizational structure should be reviewed so that any roadblocks to implementing and evaluating complementary or cross-cutting renewable energy projects can be removed (ASERTTI, 1992).

Integrating RD&D into the Broader Commercialization Process. Several new federal initiatives reflect the importance of integrating RD&D with technology commercialization. The traditional gap between DOE-sponsored laboratory research and the market has been partially closed by various technology-transfer activities: personnel exchanges, patent licensing, the shared use of lab facilities, and information dissemination. All these activities deserve continued support.

A complementary approach to incorporating market feedback in the RD&D process is to foster competition. Again, consider the example of federal support for PVs. At present, development of several types of PV cells is being supported by public funds. While all show some promise, none clearly stands out for all potential applications, so obtaining market feedback allows different types of cells to emerge as the technology of choice for different markets—depending on their longevity, reliability, cost, and efficiency requirements.

As with R&D, demonstration projects should be integrated into a broader commercialization process. Greater private-sector influence over design selection and project management, the preservation of proprietary rights, cost-sharing between government and industry, and stable and predictable public sector commitments would all promote this healthy move. So would requiring demonstration projects to translate their results into the production of salable goods. At the same time, since demonstration projects are used in part to lower perceived technological risk, they must be given the time needed to promote investor confidence (OTA, 1985).

Market-driven RD&D models have important implications for project management. Public projects need stable long-term funding if they are to provide information that allows policy-makers and investors to make more informed decisions on subsequent resource commitments. Premature decisions often make additional research necessary later and ultimately slow commercialization. But with the right information at the right time, research managers can continue, redirect, accelerate, or cancel a program on the basis of prospective costs and benefits. For this reason, a well-managed research program is likely to include projects that are cancelled after their exploratory phase (Cohen and Noll, 1991).

Improving Effectiveness of RD&D Institutions. Although public RD&D can never be completely divorced from politics, funding decisions can be better insulated from ideological and pork-barrel pressures than they are now. In particular, funding for high-cost energy technology demonstrations should be removed from the purview of Congressional committees, and DOE should come up with funding-allocation processes that maximize professional accountability through open planning and technical peer review. Any of several institutional models—some already initiated in the United States—could be used to better allocate public funds and manage programs.[49]

Cooperative Research and Development Agreements (CRADAs) are agreements between the Department of Energy (through the national labs) and private firms to support specific energy projects. CRADA guidelines call for at least 50-percent private funding. Under a CRADA, a federal lab can contribute facilities, personnel, or property to a project—but no direct funds, and the industrial partner can control any technical information generated for up to five years. To date, several CRADAs have been negotiated for renewable energy technologies, including PV, wind, and biomass. CRADA's and other mechanisms for lab/industry cooperation should be expanded and freed of red tape from DOE headquarters so small businesses can more readily take advantage of them.

Under another model, DOE would enter into for-profit partnership agreements with renewable energy firms through a financial intermediary. Projects would be selected by a professional investment manager, who would serve as a broker for negotiating parties. Projects proposed by potential DOE partners would be evaluated on the basis of four criteria: replicability, marketplace sustainability, ability to fill a market niche, and the ability to provide an acceptable return on DOE investments (Advisory Committee on Renewable Energy and Energy Efficiency Joint Ventures, 1992).

A model not yet applied to federal energy RD&D in the United States is the establishment of a revolving fund for renewable energy ventures. Government would not select the projects for funding, even though it would establish overall criteria for support, so political influence would be minimized under this scheme. Price guarantees would be provided for the sale of energy produced, and payments made to qualifying projects would be large enough to ensure adequate returns on private capital. In return for the price subsidy, government would ask for royalty shares in subsequent units of the technology that are successfully marketed. The government would manage the portfolio to break even over the long run (Kelly, Weinberg, and Williams, 1992).[50]

Another institutional model for coordinating public and private RD&D is the Japanese government's Research Institute of Innovative Technology for the Earth (RITE). Although projects are funded partly by the Ministry of International Trade and Industry (MITI), RITE is quasi-autonomous and has an environmental mandate (currently focused on alternatives to carbon fuels). The New Energy and Industrial Technology Development Organization (NEDO) is another MITI-supported R&D institution (Heaton, Repetto, and Sobin, 1992). NEDO furthers the development of technologies that emerge from public and private laboratories until the private sector commercialization efforts can take over (NEDO, 1991).

Realizing Public Procurement Opportunities

Procurement programs support market diffusion by reducing market risks and promoting production economies. Through such programs, government agencies can acquire electric or thermal applications of renewables to supply energy for their own operations or direct federal power agencies to acquire renewable electricity for resale. Public procurement can reduce unit costs as long as equipment is acquired gradually (so the program doesn't discourage efficiency improvements), competition among vendors is promoted, and contract processing is streamlined to contain time and paperwork costs.

While early federal procurement programs for renewables sometimes combined "technology-push" with "market-pull" activities, few were tied to technology-specific commercialization strategies. 1974 saw the passage of the Solar Heating and Cooling Demonstration Act, which included the first federal procurement of solar systems for testing. Another federal procurement effort materialized under the Military Construction Authorization Act of 1978, which directed the Department of Defense to use renewable technologies that were cost-effective on a life-cycle basis in all new housing and in one quarter of all other DOD buildings. Under other legislation, $98 million was authorized to equip federal facilities with photovoltaic power systems. Other early legislation incorporated procurement provisions as well, including the 1980 Wind Energy Systems and Ocean Thermal Energy Conversion Acts (Sklar, 1990). To date, however, compliance with these laws has been lax at best (Sawyer, 1986).

As the nation's largest energy consumer, the federal government's potential role in promoting renewables through procurement is immense. For example, federal power marketing agencies (PMAs) with an installed capacity of over 66,000 MW constitute a potential wholesale market for renewable energy throughout most regions of the United States. Because much of their power is ultimately delivered to rural customers, these transmission networks cover regions with tremendous renewable energy resources. The Western Area Power Administration (WAPA) territory, for example, contains wind resources in excess of WAPA's current generating capacity. The PMAs' hydroelectric facilities were constructed with federal tax support, so extending the PMAs' mandate to commercialize other indigenous resources is consistent with their original mission.

Coordinated by DOE, both PMAs and the Tennessee Valley Authority (TVA) should acquire renewable electric capacity. While law prohibits PMAs from constructing new generation facilities, they should be directed by statute to competitively acquire renewably generated power to support national commercialization objectives. As part of this effort, PMAs should construct or upgrade transmission facilities as needed to accommodate major renewable resources.

Federal agencies that don't produce energy should also establish procurement guidelines for high-volume purchases. For example, large-scale retrofits of public housing with solar water heating should be implemented where cost-effective, along with opportunities to exploit renewable resources on the Defense Department's extensive land holdings.

Local public power entities (municipal utilities, public utility districts, rural electric coops) should use procurement opportunities to drive down costs. As a precursor to volume purchases in the future, the Sacramento Municipal Utility District now offers customers PV installations at a 15-percent premium over regular rates: the PV provided portion of the customer's bill is held constant until conventional rates catch up (*The Solar Letter*, 1993). In another approach to local procurement, public utility districts in Washington state have established a joint operating agency that makes use of low-cost capital (through tax-exempt bonding) and economies of scale to reduce project costs over those incurred by individual developers (Hamrin, 1992a).

Attracting Private Investment in Commercialization

An alternative approach to direct public investment in commercializing renewable energy technology is decreasing risks or increasing returns to private investors. An advantage of this approach is that public outlays would be lower since the private sector would bear proportionally more of the costs.

Targeted Incentives

Experience with tax initiatives to overcome investment risks has demonstrated how difficult it is to craft cost-effective incentives. Tax reductions or exemptions, sales and use tax exemptions, income tax deductions, and income tax credits have all initially seemed effective in mobilizing private investment. Indeed, estimates of real rates of return under various scenarios based on federal tax incentives available in 1985 range from 9 to 28 percent, depending on technology, compared to 0 to 12 percent with no tax incentives (OTA, 1985). But over the long term, such incentives often have not created lasting markets. *(See Box VI-3.)*

Avoiding the shortcomings of previous incentive mechanisms. Past tax incentives have been less than effective for many reasons. First, most programs weren't consistent or predictable enough over time to induce long-term cost reductions. For instance, in the 1970s and early 1980s many firms entered the tax-enhanced market for solar-thermal equipment. Because fixed costs were substantial, each new manufacturer had to maintain some minimum scale of output to remain competitive. When the residential solar tax credits expired

Box VI-3. Tax Incentives for Renewable Energy

Tax Exemptions. A property tax exemption removes the property tax liability for renewable energy equipment but does not affect its upfront purchase price. As of 1992, thirteen states offered property tax exemptions for specific renewable energy equipment. Sales tax exemptions lower the price of renewable energy equipment at the time of purchase. Four states offered such exemptions as of 1992.

The California property tax exemption has been significant in making solar electric generating plants attractive to investors. Property taxes represent about 10 percent of the annual revenue of the plants. Without this exemption, plant owners would pay about four times the taxes owed on a gas-fired plant of comparable size (Lotker, 1991).

Tax Credits. A tax credit is a direct deduction from taxes due of a percentage of the expenditure for eligible items. The first renewable energy tax law, the Energy Tax Act of 1976, allowed homeowners to deduct from their taxes 40 percent of the cost of solar space and water heating equipment, for a maximum credit of $10,000. The same law provided a 10-percent solar business investment tax credit through December 31, 1982 (Sklar, 1990).[1] Commercial tax credits were also enacted for solar and wind systems. Under the Windfall Profits Tax Act of 1980, the business tax credit was raised to 15 percent and extended through December 1, 1985. Later, the commercial tax credits for solar, geothermal, and ocean thermal technology were extended through December 31, 1988, but the solar business tax credit was reduced to 10 percent. In 1988, the solar business credit was extended for another year. In 1989, the business tax credit for solar thermal, photovoltaic, and geothermal energy was stretched until December 31, 1991, at 10 percent. In 1991, it was extended through the first half of 1992 (Sklar, 1990), and in 1992 it received a permanent extension.

The 1992 energy legislation also created a 1.5 cents/kWh production tax credit (PTC) for wind and "dedicated" biomass. Unlike early tax credits based on capital investment, the PTC awards credits based on energy generated. Its direct effect will be to increase the after-tax returns to investors in wind and biomass projects (Oberg, 1992).[2]

Among the ten states that offered tax credits as of 1992, some credits cover a comprehensive range of renewable energy devices. Montana, for example, allows solar, wind, solid waste, decomposition of organic waste as a fuel source, some passive solar, and systems that generate electricity from wood wastes, hydropower, and geothermal energy. Hawaii offers a credit for multi-family buildings of 35 percent of system cost or $350 per residential unit, whichever is less. North Carolina offers tax credits against corporate income tax—for solar hot water and cooling, photovoltaics, wind, solar thermal for process heat, and other renewable energy devices—ranging from 10 to 30 percent of cost.

Accelerated Depreciation. This provision increases an independent power producer's returns in the early years of production. While tax reforms in 1986 increased the depreciation period for non-utility generation projects to 15 to 31 years, property used to tap solar, wind, geothermal, ocean energy, and biomass (municipal solid waste) remains depreciable over five years at 200 percent (using the declining balance method). Other tax benefits are available to both renewable and nonrenewable independent power projects, depending on ownership, fuel, financing, and location (Ferry, 1990).

---

1. The business tax credit has specific limitations. The credit is not allowed against the minimum alternative tax. Unused credits can be carried back 3 years and forward 15 years. For depreciation and other purposes, the basis of eligible property is reduced by 50 percent of the credit allowed, regardless of whether the taxpayer has received any actual tax benefit from the credit. Taxpayers paying the minimum tax receive depreciation deductions for solar energy property that are less generous than if solar credits were not available. In computing minimum tax liability, the tax credit is not allowed and depreciation of solar energy property is calculated using a 12-year life. Because many investors in solar power production pay only the minimum tax, these provisions may limit the investor pool and increase the yields needed to attract investors.

2. Because of restrictions in the tax code, the PTC will generate somewhat less than the full 1.5 cent/kWh cost decrease for eligible projects.

(Sklar, 1990), domestic sales fell from $900 million in 1985 to $300 million in 1986 (Sissine, 1990), and the number of manufacturers and installers contracted proportionally. In fact, the solar industry was actually smaller in 1986 than it was before federal tax credits were initiated. Even while the tax credit was in effect, so many firms entered the market that the average per-firm output was limited and potential cost reductions from longer production runs and experience were sacrificed. Meanwhile, the implementation of state incentives has been inconsistent too. In 1984, some 30 states had business or residential tax credits or had deductions for renewable energy systems; by 1991, only 12 states offered them. In 1984, ten states exempted renewable energy equipment from sales tax or offered refunds. In 1991, only four did (NATAS, 1992; Sawyer and Lancaster, 1985).

Second, tax credits based on capital costs gave manufacturers and developers incentives to goldplate designs for equipment—some of it inefficient. Producers, suppliers, and installers may have been less cost-conscious and consumers less price-sensitive than they would have been without tax credits. In the worst cases, technology with no chance of commercial success was installed (OTA, 1985).

Third, past tax incentives had only limited influence on investment decisions. According to one simulation analysis, the business investment tax credit did little to influence investment decisions for the renewable energy projects surveyed[51] (U.S. GAO, 1983).

Crafting Incentives as Part of Commercialization Plans. The 1992 Production Tax Credit (PTC) for wind and "dedicated" or "closed loop" biomass projects does avoid some of the problems inherent in past tax subsidies, particularly the incentive to goldplate product designs. But in its current form, this credit is poorly matched to eligible technologies and poorly coordinated with other policies. In the case of biomass, the PTC is premature as a market stimulus. Whether or not 1.5 cents/kWh would make electricity from closed loop biomass technologies competitive—an open question—the growing, harvesting, transporting, and (for some fuel cycles) gasifying of different feedstocks are still nascent arts. Certainly most producers of power from this source are in no position to take advantage of the PTC. And since the PTC expires in 1999, there isn't time enough for further research and testing, especially of rotations of woody biomass. Moreover, the credit is available only when power is generated, so potential feedstock producers face the risk that market demand for these new products will be slack or erratic.

On the other hand, wind technologies and markets are poised to make use of the PTC. But in this case too, the cost-effectiveness of the PTC will depend on how much new investment it stimulates to further reduce the cost of wind energy.

Overall, experience with tax incentives for renewables suggests several important guidelines that would enhance their cost-effectiveness:

- Tax subsidies should be targeted at particular renewable energy technologies only if they serve an explicitly defined social objective (such as reducing the cost of energy produced by renewable energy equipment) more cost-effectively than do alternative policy tools.
- The long-term effectiveness of tax subsidies should be evaluated in terms of whether the economic signals they send to subsidy recipients and other stakeholders (such as capital markets) clearly promote their identified objectives.
- Tax subsidies should be implemented only as part of a commercialization strategy and should reflect the current stage of commercial development of eligible technologies.
- While subsidies might buffer precommercial technologies from volatile market conditions—a valid function—they should not be so large that they insulate the targeted technologies from all market competition.
- Tax subsidies should have sunset provisions. Incentives should diminish over time as the technology matures and investment risks decrease.
- Both utilities and independent power producers should be eligible for tax incentives.

Reducing Investment Risks

While renewable equipment suppliers face market risks, purchasers of renewable equipment run the risk—associated with trying any new technology—that performance problems will arise. Because the commercial viability of a technology depends on how well it works in its intended surroundings, a firm might not find out that a technology is infeasible until after it is put to work. For example, a major variable in the cost of energy from wind is materials fatigue over the 20-to-30-year service life of turbine blades, but modern wind machines haven't been around for three decades yet (Committee on Assessment of Research Needs for Wind Turbine Rotor Materials Technology et al., 1991).

Safe Harbor Rules. As electric generation is deregulated, utilities' incentive to invest in commercially immature technologies decreases, leaving the investor's role to independent developers. Yet, utilities can generally identify and analyze ways to integrate renewables into their systems better than independent developers can. *(See Chapter IV.)* Unfortunately, utilities' fear of regulatory reprisal for the financial loss associated with technical failure limits their experimentation with any technologies not yet proven in utility applications. To realize the large potential of utility-built renewable capacity, utilities clearly need the chance to become more familiar with new technologies.

Key questions for utilities include:
- Will the new facility come on-line at its anticipated capacity rating?
- Will the technology cost more to construct or operate than anticipated?
- Will construction be completed late because of technical or regulatory problems?
- Will the technology be significantly less reliable than planned?
- Will its life-time be shorter than expected—due either to technical problems or unanticipated regulatory decisions?

Under pressure to hold down rates in the short run, regulators often question the benefits of R&D expenditures. For example, Green Mountain Power was recently told it could not recover R&D costs for wind machines. Periodically, Pacific Gas and Electric's expenditures on R&D are challenged on grounds that they subsidize future PG&E ratepayers or those outside of PG&E's service area rather than current ratepayers, and substantial cost recovery for PG&E's renewable energy R&D programs was recently disallowed (McCormack, 1993). The more technology-related risks that shareholders have to bear, the less likely utilities are to experiment with renewables—or exotic fossil fuel technologies, for that matter.

Utility investment in renewable energy projects could be encouraged by state PUC regulations that partially protect stockholders. By setting permissible boundaries for utility experimentation and allowing full cost recovery for well-conceived and well-managed demonstration projects, utilities can gain experience with renewables within a "safe harbor." At the same time, such rules offer an effective means of limiting overall investments to levels that protect ratepayer interests. Safe-harbor rules might specify the types of projects, the scale of any single project, the aggregate scale of all projects combined, and the maximum duration of allowed cost recovery. Of course, these rules should not be used to protect shareholders from normal energy-supply investment risks. Also, to the extent that some information benefits from ratepayer-supported projects spill outside a utility's service area, support from government or utility consortia needs to be expanded to make sure that the information costs are similarly spread around. In particular, the utility industry's research arm (EPRI) should increase the share of its budget devoted to renewables beyond the current 7 percent (U.S. GAO, 1993).

Collaborative Acquisitions. A one-of-a-kind renewable project will usually cost a utility more than an installation that represents part of a sustained and increasing stream of orders. While multiple acquisitions by individual utilities might reduce costs, in most cases aggregating markets would cut them farther. Aggregating markets for renewables regionally or nationally could help achieve and maintain cost reductions.

Although individual utilities have little incentive to aggregate markets, the utility industry as a whole does. One approach is for a group of utilities to issue a "Notice of Market Opportunity" that offers the winner of a competition a volume purchase for commercializing a specific renewable application. The risks to manufacturers of expanding capacity would drop along with those to the first purchasers, who would receive royalties from the sale of future lower-cost units. Public and private utilities are trying this approach to commercialization for urban applications of fuel-cell technology (Douglas, 1991).

Somewhat modified approaches may be more appropriate for technologies that require both technical improvements and guaranteed markets. An EPA program called Golden Carrots links appliance manufacturers with utilities to stimulate technical innovation and address the "chicken/egg" problem as it applies to the development and adoption of high-efficiency appliances. In this program, a competitive RFP is issued to appliance manufacturers for a model that exceeds current state-of-the-art efficiency, with funds provided by a consortium of utilities. A guaranteed market is available to the winning manufacturer since the utilities will use the product in their demand-management programs.

This general collaborative concept appears most applicable to PV's and other renewable technologies whose costs decline rapidly with production increases (Sachs et al., 1993). Government can help form these alliances by bringing together the relevant stakeholders on neutral territory and by paying part of the up-front costs. Public expenditures may be limited to the costs associated with forming and maintaining the alliance. Alternatively, government may help "buy down" the temporary gap between equipment producers' costs and users' willingness-to-pay, as recently proposed for PVs by a utility consortium.

Export Promotion. Export promotion—whether through direct channels or buy-back provisions in development assistance—has been used mainly to help U.S. renewable energy producers improve or maintain world market share, thereby helping the U.S. trade balance. *(See Table VI-3.)* During the Reagan Administration, Congress established an interagency task force called the Committee on Renewable Energy Commerce and Trade (CORECT) to promote exports of renewable energy equipment. CORECT's effectiveness is measured by the sale of U.S. renewable energy products and services resulting from its promotional activities. 1992 legislation expanded CORECT's responsibilities by calling for the creation of a database on developing countries' renewable energy needs and the establishment of foreign outreach offices. Another law (the Foreign Operations, Export Financing, and Related Programs Appropriations Act of 1990) calls for U.S.-supported multilateral development banks and the Agency for International Development to increase the number of staff experts in renewable energy technologies and to promote renewable energy in loan-making or grant-giving (Sissine, 1990). This law also directs the Export-Import Bank to spend 5 percent of all energy sector export-promotion funds on renewable energy (Sklar, 1990).

States are also pushing exports of energy equipment on their own. According to a recent survey for the National Association of State Energy Officials, 88 percent of the responding states have an international trade-development program to help businesses export technologies. Thirty-five percent help only those companies that manufacture or provide renewable energy and energy-efficiency technologies and related services. On the other hand, only five states have successfully marketed renewable energy technologies abroad (National Association of State Energy Officials, 1991). Of these, California, whose Energy Technology Export program provides technical assistance to companies selling products and services abroad (Interstate Solar Coordination Council, 1991), and Arizona, which also provides assistance for energy businesses to export (Solar Industry Journal, 1992), have the largest programs.

While individual firms have undoubtedly been helped along, past export promotion has not necessarily made the U.S. renewable energy industry more competitive over the long run. The true determinants of international competitiveness—fully consistent with domestic commercialization objectives—are improved product quality or production efficiency, not just sales.

Since major U.S. competitors use both export promotion and "tied aid" (the practice of establishing markets abroad by requiring that some percentage of development assistance be spent on services and equipment from the donor countries), calls to expand federal export-promotion activities for renewable technologies are heard often. But any such export-promotion activities should be directly tied to commercialization objectives for specific technologies. All such activities should aim to create a steady aggregate demand that encourages increases in manufacturing capacity. In addition, opportunities for lowering the costs of entering foreign markets should be exploited before more costly and potentially trade-distorting measures—such as loan subsidies—are tried.

	Export-Import Bank of the U.S.	Overseas Private Investment Corporation
Table VI-3. Export Promotion Services Offered by Agency		
Prefeasibility Study Funds		
Feasibility Study Funds	X	
Direct Loans	X	
Loan Guarantees	X	X
Other	X	X

Source: U.S. Export Council for Renewable Energy, 1992.

Developing Coordinated Commercialization Plans

If past government efforts to commercialize renewable energy technologies have met with only limited success, what's to be done now to address current barriers to commercialization? Short of specifying the optimal nature and level of public investment for each renewable technology, it is possible to establish broad guidelines for public policy and investment decisions. Four are particularly important:

1. Develop Commercialization Plans

The ultimate goal of technology commercialization is the creation of a sustainable competitive market for a product. A commercialization plan should thus take account of the current commercial status of a technology, establish realistic quantitative objectives (for efficiency, production costs, or market penetration, etc.) that pro-

U.S. Trade and Development Program	U.S. Agency for International Development	Small Business Administration
X	X	
X	X	
		X
	X	X

mote the long-term goal, and identify government actions that will complement private investments to achieve the objectives.

Any such plan should provide a basis for choosing among various policy tools to achieve stated goals at the lowest cost possible. There is no single way to evaluate the success of public support for private-sector commercialization across different technologies. Different measures of success (conversion efficiency, cost of energy, return on investment, market share, firm survival, and market entry rates, etc.) may need to be applied at different stages of the development cycle (Brown and Wilson, 1992). Moreover, a policy may help subsidized firms get a foothold in new markets without necessarily improving national welfare (Ford and Suyker, 1990). Thus, when policy-makers consider two or more ways of promoting the same commercialization objective, the anticipated cost-effectiveness of each should be evaluated from both budgetary and social accounting perspectives.

Commercialization plans should also provide for systematic feedback and correction during policy implementation. Varied federal and state renewable energy programs throughout the 1980s constituted a laboratory for alternative policy approaches, but policy-makers weren't able to learn from this experience because nobody evaluated it systematically and objectively. (*See*, for example, Rich and Roessner, 1990.) From now on, program managers must supplement anecdotes and "bean counting" with independent evaluation of the cost-effectiveness of renewable energy commercialization efforts.

2. Involve Appropriate Actors in Policy Implementation

A group of stakeholders may either benefit from or bear the risks of technology-commercialization investments, or both. For a given investment, stakeholders might include utility ratepayers, utility shareholders, building owners, or individuals who receive environmental benefits from a local or regional shift to renewable resource use. Such groups should be invited to help develop and implement commercialization plans. Similarly, if both public and private investment in research and development is required, overall returns to society are likely to increase.

Such collaboration among stakeholders is emerging as an important factor in renewables deployment (Birk, 1992). Indeed, several cooperative consortia have recently been created to overcome commercialization barriers. One group, formed to promote utility applications of PVs, includes manufacturers, utilities, state regulators and energy officials, consumer advocates, and the federal government (Weissman, 1992). Utilities, wind-turbine vendors, and the federal government are also working together to commercialize the next generation of turbines. A DOE-sponsored collaborative brought together building-industry representatives and lenders to address barriers to implementing energy efficiency and renewable energy applications in buildings (NREL, 1992). Finally, representatives from the utility industry, agricultural and forestry interests, and the environmental community have been developing principles for sustainable biomass energy systems. While it may be premature to judge these collaborative efforts, all recognize the benefits of coordination among key stakeholders.

148

By providing financial support, the federal government can catalyze market-led collaborations that both benefit stakeholders and promote its own commercialization objectives. Because market aggregation works best at the national level for many technologies, even large states may not have markets large enough to bring down unit costs. Also, many environmental effects mitigated by renewables cross state boundaries. In addition, energy consumers in any region stand to benefit from state or utility-level commercialization activities that reduce the cost of renewables, and the federal government is uniquely positioned to share and spread the risks associated with new technologies.

Of course, national commercialization strategies must reflect the fact that the value of renewable energy varies by location and application. States and localities are better able than the federal government to identify and match renewable energy sources with high-value demands, and—with regulatory leverage over the mix of generation resources acquired by private utilities—state PUCs must be principal actors in efforts to overcome the technological and market risks facing renewable energy development. However, so that mandated utility acquisitions of precommercial technologies don't force individual states or utilities to subsidize the rest of the country, the utility industry as a whole (through trade and research organizations such as the Electric Power Research Institute) and the federal government should shoulder the major share of needed investments.

3. Target and Implement Policy Instruments

How cost effective any policy instrument is depends in good measure on whether it has been keyed to a technology's stage of commercialization. *(See Box IV-4.)* Early solar tax credits intended to stimulate demand for market-ready technologies were applied prematurely (Rich and Roessner, 1990). At the other extreme, money will also be wasted if a subsidy is applied to technology that is already competitive in most circumstances.

Technology-targeted incentives and other policies should be long-lasting and predictable enough to secure investments. If the goal is to achieve realistic cost targets, sunset provisions shouldn't come into effect until production economies can be achieved. Nor should incentives be terminated abruptly. Since their consistency and pre-

Box VI-4. Commercialization Barriers Faced by Various
Renewable Energy Technologies

Each renewable energy technology may require a different commercialization strategy based on different policies. For all renewables, though, the stage of commercial development is a key factor.

Biomass

Biomass electric generation already uses relatively mature generating technologies. But large-scale dedicated biomass production for electricity or gasification faces significant barriers in feedstock development due to current federal agricultural policy, landowners' well-grounded fear of committing acreage for several years to a commodity whose future demand is uncertain, and long-term resource and environmental risks.

Geothermal

The costs of discovering resources and drilling must be lowered and better methods for prolonging the life of resources developed. For hot dry rock, water must be available for injecting into the rock to extract heat, and energy flows from rock fissures must last long enough to justify extraction costs.

Hydropower

Although hydropower is in many respects a mature technology, research is needed to increase the efficiency and reliability of hydro facilities, decrease maintenance costs, and mitigate environmental impacts.

Passive Solar

Successful commercialization of passive solar requires little new technology, but depends on educating a broad range of building professionals. In particular, the effective application of passive solar concepts requires special attention to the details of building design and construction. Also, techniques for integrating new technologies into whole-building design (including heat transfer, air circulation, and human comfort) remain a constraint.

dictability may ultimately be more important than their size, subsidies should be phased out according to an announced schedule.

4. Replicate Successful Strategies

While parts of commercialization strategies have been developed for several renewable energy technologies, the strategy for PVs appears as currently the most complete. *(See Box VI-5.)* Key facets of the PV strategy are the development of a technology-specific plan with clearly defined goals and targets, risk-sharing among key stakeholders, evaluation of alternative initiatives according to how well they are expected to achieve commercialization objectives, and phased implementation of initiatives based on each application's stage of commercial maturity. This strategy should be monitored closely so that appropriate elements can be adapted to other renewable technologies.

Box VI-5. PV Commercialization Strategy

National Coordination. The Department of Energy has developed a broad PV commercialization strategy, "Solar 2000," to facilitate more focused commercialization efforts: technology development, improvements in manufacturing, and accelerated market development.

Development of technology-specific initiatives. The PV strategy is based on the recognition that market penetration can be accelerated either through decline in unit costs or increase in acceptable prices (through high-value applications). As they penetrate high-value niche markets, manufacturers will increasingly be able to invest in the expansion of production facilities. In turn, expanding production capacity drives down costs to open up broader markets (Weissman, 1992). The strategy identifies alternative approaches to boost utilities' confidence in the technology and get them to incorporate high-value applications into their power systems. Similarly, the strategy identifies ways of assuring manufacturers of market demand.

Box VI-5. (continued)

Involvement of key stakeholders. The utility stakeholders currently comprise a group of about 40 utilities (the Utility Photovoltaic Group) interested in approaching commercialization from the perspective of potential PV buyers (utilities). It is complemented by the "Photovoltaics for Utilities" initiative: together, public and private utility organizations, state regulatory and consumer groups, and the PV industry met to develop specific action steps that each should take (Weissman, 1993). To share risks, these stakeholders all commit resources to the program. A consensus among stakeholders is being developed on which approaches should be taken to accelerate market penetration. All options include competition among multiple suppliers and management of risks between early buyers and suppliers, and are based on volume purchases driven by buyer needs.

Timing initiatives to take each technology's phase of commercial development into account. The Utility PV Group has identified two commercialization tracks to follow simultaneously. One is promoting currently cost-effective applications through information and education efforts directed at utilities. The other is accelerating high-value applications by increasing utilities' awareness of them, developing appropriate analytical tools for evaluating applications, and deciding upon and implementing strategies to encourage high-volume PV purchases (Utility PhotoVoltaic Group, 1992; Weissman, 1992).

Keith Lee Kozloff is a Senior Associate in the Climate, Energy, and Pollution Program at the World Resources Institute, where he is currently evaluating policies for renewable energy in developing countries. Previously, Dr. Kozloff worked for six years in the state of Minnesota's energy office. **Roger C. Dower** is currently Director of the Climate, Energy, and Pollution Program at WRI. Prior to coming to WRI, he was Chief of the Energy and Environment Unit at the Congressional Budget Office, U.S. Congress.

APPENDICES

Appendix A. Summaries of Renewable Energy Technologies[52]

Photovoltaics

Photovoltaic cells convert (PVs) solar radiation directly into electricity. Each cell contains two layers of semiconductor material; one treated to have a positive charge and the other, a negative charge. When excited by photons, electrons flow from the negatively charged material to the positively charged semi-conducting material, creating a current. As shown in Table A-1, the major end uses of photovoltaics are consumer products, remote applications, and utility generation. The supply of photovoltaic grid-connected power in the United States increased from 1 MWe in 1982 to 13 MWe in 1989.

PV cell prices have been dropping while conversion efficiency has increased. As a result, the cost of solar electricity decreased from $1.50/kWh in 1980 (U.S. DOE, Five Year Research Plan, 1987–1991, National Photovoltaics Program, p. 5) to $.20–$.30 in 1991 (OTA, 1991). Engineers have also succeeded in increasing the lifetimes of PV systems, and they anticipate 30-year lifespans for current versions. Balance-of-system technology (all the equipment required for a PV system that is not part of the PV module), such as utility grid interconnection equipment, dc-to-ac inverters, and support structures, has also become much better understood over the last ten years.

Photovoltaics are expected to penetrate increasingly large market niches as the cost of PV-generated energy drops. PV technologies tend to be differentiated according to trade-offs between effi-

Table A-1. U.S. Module Shipments by Market Sector (MegaWatts)

Application	1986	1987	1988	1989	1990	1991	1992
Grid-Connected	0.5	0.2	0.6	0.4	0.4	0.2	0.8
Central Station (1MW)	–	–	–	–	–	–	–
Exports	3.8	4.7	5.5	5.9	6.4	9.0	9.2
Off-Grid Residential	0.6	1.5	2.2	2.5	2.8	2.6	2.6
Government Projects	0.3	0.05	0.2	0.5	0.5	0.5	0.8
Off-Grid Industrial and Commercial	1.4	1.6	2.0	2.3	2.5	2.4	2.9
Consumer Products (Less than 10W)	0.5	0.6	0.8	2.5	2.2	2.4	2.2
Total	**7.1**	**8.65**	**11.3**	**14.1**	**14.8**	**17.1**	**18.5**

Source: Maycock, 1993.

ciency and cost per KW. At the moment, no PV technology is a clear standout for all applications. *(See Table A-2.)*

Thermal Electric Technologies

Solar thermal plants produce electricity by concentrating sunlight onto a working fluid or engine. Parabolic troughs, for example, concentrate sunlight as much as 80-fold onto a tube (a "line source") at the focal line of the trough. A working fluid, usually water or oil, circulates through the tube, captures the heat, and transports it to the point of use. Concentrator systems can be used by utilities to generate bulk power, and some thermal-electric technologies are appropriate for small scale uses, such as parabolic

Table A-2. Average Price of Photovoltaic Cells and Percent of Total Shipments by Cell Type, 1990

Type	Weighted Average Price ($/Peak Watt)		Percent of Total Shipments
	Modules	Cells	
Crystalline Silicon			
Single-Crystal	5.66	3.96	54
Cast and Ribbon	5.68	3.41	36
Subtotal	5.67	3.87	90
Thin Film Amorphous			
Silicon	5.65	2.00	10
Concentrator Silicon	12.28	13.77	<0.5
Total	**5.68**	**3.84**	**100**

Source: PV News, 1992.

dish/Stirling engine systems. Parabolic dishes resemble troughs but focus sunlight onto a point.

Parabolic troughs are the most mature of the solar-thermal technologies, producing 90 percent of the world's solar electricity. Under limited circumstances, troughs are cost-competitive for industrial uses and utility peak and intermediate power. Capital costs have dropped from $4,000 per kilowatt to $2,000 per kilowatt for the only substantial solar trough installation in the United States, a hybrid system in which natural gas supplements solar energy. *(See Figure A-1.)*

Central receiver systems have fields of mirrors called heliostats that focus sunlight onto a single central receiver, which is mounted on a tower. These systems are not yet commercially available, but some manufacturing capability exists. Currently, six demonstration plants worldwide have an installed capacity of 11 megawatts.

Concentrating collectors have been improved in the last ten years. Piping systems have become more reliable, and thermal performance has improved. Computer tracking systems have also become more reliable and have been perfected for troughs. Research

155

Figure A-1: Solar Electric Generation Cost Reduction

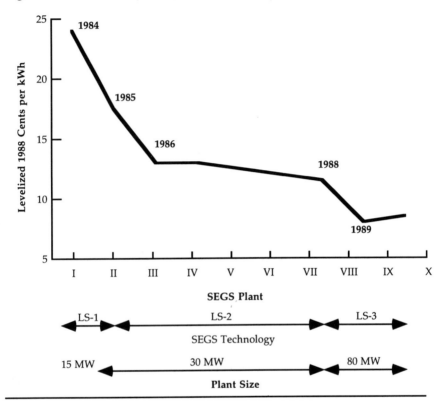

Source: Lotker, 1991

is still needed to reduce capital costs by developing lower cost, higher performance, and longer-lived collectors. Thermal losses must also be reduced.

Wind Power

Wind machines convert the kinetic energy of wind into rotational energy that drives electricity-generating turbines. Wind turbines have either vertical or horizontal axes. The more common horizontal axis turbines are like the windmills of old, with propeller-like blades mounted on a tower, and yaw control systems that keep the rotor pointed into the wind. Vertical axis wind turbines resemble huge eggbeaters, with two or three curved blades attached to the top and bottom of a vertical shaft.

Wind turbines are used primarily to generate electricity. More than 17,000 wind turbines are operating in the United States, and by late 1991 they had generated about 13 billion kWh in California. While wind capacity remains concentrated in California, (See Figure A-2) facilities are being planned for the Northwest, Midwest, and New England.

The cost of wind power has fallen dramatically during the past decade. For utility-scale turbines, a kWh cost $0.68 in 1980 but only $0.06 by 1990 (Larson et al., 1992), and next-generation utility-scale machines are projected to produce power at $0.05/kWh. Mass-production techniques, siting improvements, standardization, and scheduling maintenance during times of slack wind account for most of the savings to date. Significant technological improvements include new blade designs and variable speed turbines.

Solar-Thermal Collectors

The principle behind flat-plate solar collectors for thermal energy is the same as for other direct solar applications, but the technology is simpler. Fluid exposed to the sun absorbs solar radiation. The efficiency of solar collection is enhanced by running the fluid through tubes optically coated for maximum solar absorption and by placing the tubes and plate inside a glazed but otherwise insulated box. The energy thus collected is stored, as in a hot-water tank. Most solar thermal applications are backed up by other space- or water-heating systems.

Standardization and shake-out in the industry during the 1980s have resulted in higher-quality, more reliable solar collector systems. Performance has been improved greatly by better absorber designs, more effective insulation, and advanced selective surfaces. Efficiency increased about 30 percent between 1977 and the mid-1980s.

As Table A-3 shows, the current market for solar-thermal collectors is dominated by swimming pool uses and domestic water heating. Growth potential in other market segments is substantial, however. For example, advances in solar water-heating systems

Figure A-2: California Wind Power Plants Capacity Installed

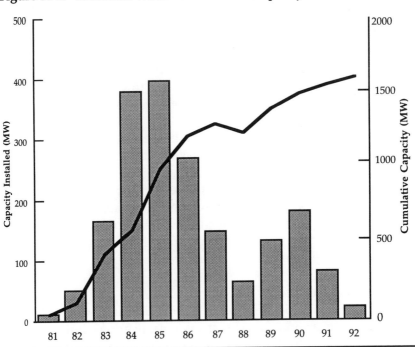

Source: AWEA,1991.

and lowered space-heating requirements through efficiency measures offer the potential for using a combined solar collector system to heat both water and space.

Passive Solar

Passive solar uses elements of building design rather than mechanical systems to capture and store solar energy for heating, cooling, ventilation, and lighting. The primary features of a passive solar building are typically south-facing glazing and thermal mass—placed and sized to take advantage of such natural processes as conduction, convection, and radiation to maintain comfortable temperatures. Depending on the region, passive solar design can provide 50 to 80 percent of building-heating requirements in the United States (Givoni, 1991).

Current passive solar designs include several types of systems. In direct-gain systems, the sun shines directly into the space to be heated, usually onto thermal mass. Indirect gain systems have the thermal mass located adjacent to the area to be heated. Passive techniques can also be used to cool homes and buildings. A simple application of passive solar heating and cooling principles is earth-sheltered construction. Daylighting (using natural light as much as possible) is another important application of passive solar design since the largest portion of electricity use in many large buildings is neither heating nor cooling, but lighting. It is estimated that over 200,000 homes and 15,000 non-residential buildings employed passive solar designs by 1985 (REI, 1986, p. 183), with relatively little passively-designed construction since then.

Table A-3. Shipments of Solar Thermal Collectors by End Use and Sector, 1991

End Use	1,000 Square Feet
Pool Heating	5,535
Water Heating	989
Space Heating	24
Combined Space and Water Heating	8
Space Cooling	2
Process Heating	12
Other	1
Total	**6,573**

Market Sector	
Residential	6,322
Commercial	225
Industrial	13
Other	13
Total	**6,573**

Source: EIA Survey cited in *The Solar Letter*, 12-25-92.

In most parts of the country, passive solar commercial and residential buildings are cost-competitive with conventionally heated and cooled buildings because many design features can be built in at little or no extra cost. Researchers continue to develop new technologies (such as variable emissivity windows) that enhance the flexibility of passive solar designs to maintain comfortable temperatures in a wide range of climates and weather. Recent glazing technologies offer the potential for opening the enormous building-retrofit market to passive solar design.

Biomass

Solid biomass combustion is used for both heating and electricity. The primary sources of biomass for electricity production are wood, wood wastes, and wood byproducts, but agricultural wastes and municipal solid wastes are also important sources. Most biomass-fired electricity comes from non-utility generators with easy access to these forms of biomass. To burn solid biomass, conventional steam boiler technology is used. Municipal solid waste can be burned in a minimally processed state in "mass burn" facilities.

Direct combustion is cost-competitive at suitable locations if the biomass is available within about 50 miles of the powerplant (OTA, 1991; CEC, 1991). Research efforts are being devoted to growing both trees (short-rotation hardwoods) and herbaceous plants for combustion.

While most biomass fuels are harvested in solid form, methane is recovered from landfills, manure and sewage treatment facilities, and food-processing plants. Technology for anaerobic digestion is commercially available and cost-effective in restricted circumstances. Biomass can also be processed into liquid fuels.

Geothermal Energy

Geothermal energy is heat trapped up to 3,000 feet below Earth's surface. The resource is found in four different forms: hydrothermal energy (steam, hot water, or hot brine of at least 90°C and located within 900 feet of the earth's surface); hot brine under pressure that contains dissolved natural gas, otherwise known as geopressurized brine; magma, which is molten rock; and hot dry rock.

At present, hydrothermal energy is the primary geothermal resource that is used commercially. Low- and moderate-temperature hydrothermal energy (50–180°C) is much more abundant than high-temperature hydrothermal. The former can be used for space and industrial process heat, district heating, heat and hot water for such large buildings as schools and hospitals, and a variety of industrial uses in the food, chemical, and wood product industries (IEA, 1987). Geothermal steam from vapor-dominated reservoirs (up to 300°C) drives steam turbines that generate electricity.

Hydrothermal technology is considered fully mature. In California, 63 power plants provided 3160 megawatts in 1990 (CEC, 1991, p. 1.3.1.1). While some observers classify geothermal as a renewable energy source, at The Geysers, a major geothermal complex in California, power production is falling by as much as 11 percent per year on certain leases. This problem reflects inadequate understanding of long-term geothermal output and the open access nature of the resource. *(See Figure A-3.)*

A hybrid technology that uses geothermal or solar heat is the ground-source heat pump. In this technology, the solar or geothermal heated thermal mass of the ground is used instead of outside air to either extract or dissipate heat, depending on the season. This makes the ground source heat pump cost-effective, especially in new construction, over a wider geographic range than conventional heat pumps.

Hydropower

Waterpower was a mainstay of the industrial revolution in the United States, and today it is by far the most important renewable resource used for electric generation. Depending on annual rainfall, it can produce up to 14 percent of all electricity generated in the United States. Hydroelectric technologies are often divided by size into two categories.[53] Small-scale hydro facilities are generally defined, as in PURPA, as those with 30 MW or less of installed capacity. Plants with more than 30 MW are considered large-scale and range up to the 6,100-MW Grand Coulee Dam. Hydropower capacity and potential is concentrated in the Northwest, the Colorado Basin, the Tennessee Valley, and New York state.

161

Figure A-3: Cumulative Installed U.S. Hydrothermal Capacity

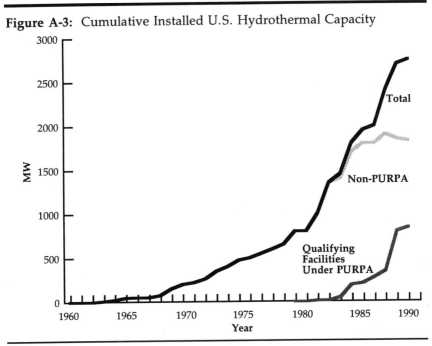

Source: Energy Information Administration, 1991.

Until 1930, most hydro plants were built by industry or utilities. This changed during the Depression, when many federal projects were built. From 1950 to 1975, hydro capacity roughly tripled. As shown in Figure A-4, the growth of hydro capacity additions has recently slowed. Further development is expected to be modest through 2000.

While hydropower is a mature technology, efficiency can be improved by using new materials, optimizing turbines for low-head projects, and upgrading old plants. New deployment modes, such as ultra low-head and in-stream turbines, can be further developed. Particularly needed is further research on environmental mitigation techniques, especially those for reducing impacts on fish.

Figure A-4: Cumulative U.S. Hydro Capacity

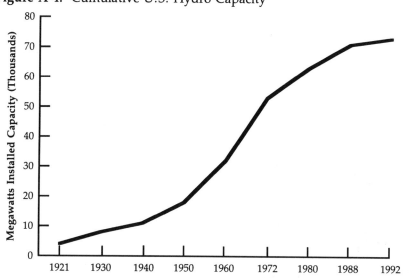

Source: FERC, 1988

Ocean Energy

Ocean thermal energy conversion (OTEC) exploits the difference between the temperature of the warm surface waters and the cooler waters 2000 to 3000 feet down to drive an engine to generate electricity. Closed-cycle OTEC power systems run a working fluid through an evaporator, where warm surface water vaporizes the working fluid. Next, the vaporized fluid drives a turbogenerator. Finally, the fluid re-condenses to a liquid in a condenser cooled by water from the depths (IEA, 1987, p. 280). OTEC engines operate inefficiently because the thermal gradients between surface layers and lower depths are very small. While OTEC is a potential source of baseload electricity, OTEC systems are still in the R&D stage. No commercial suppliers exist.

Other ocean technologies can harness the mechanical energy of waves to produce electricity. "Surface followers" convert the up-and-down motion of waves into electricity by means of a mechanical connection to a fixed pivot. Tidal power generates electricity

163

using the same principle as hydropower, capturing water from the rising and falling tides and forcing it through a turbine (REI, 1986). Wave-energy systems are neither cost-competitive nor commercially available within the United States, though two foreign companies have reportedly sold systems abroad. Tidal energy systems, potentially a source of baseload electricity, are not commercially available in the United States, and the technology is not cost-competitive.

Integrative and Storage Technologies
Several technologies facilitate the integration of renewable energy technologies into existing energy systems. First, storage technologies can help increase the value of intermittent renewables, especially in on-site applications.

• *Batteries* store excess electricity in the form of chemical energy. For renewable electricity in utility systems, battery storage in modular units would accommodate demand during peak hours or at times when renewable electricity is not otherwise available. Various new battery types are being developed to improve energy density, life, and capacity, thereby reducing the cost of energy storage.

• *Superconducting magnetic energy storage* relies on the conduction of electricity with virtually no resistance at extremely low temperatures. Energy is stored as direct current flowing through a coil or, alternatively, as the magnetic field associated with that current. While still in the research and development phase, certain ceramics have been discovered to be superconducting at higher temperatures, allowing liquid nitrogen to replace the more costly liquid hydrogen or helium as coolant.

• *Thermal storage* is a way of banking enough solar energy so that it can be used as the main or only source of heat for hot water or space heat. Storage volume must be sufficient so that all solar energy collected but not used immediately can be kept available without causing overheating. Seasonal storage has been used in housing developments, multi-family housing, and commercial buildings. Thermal storage, such as with molten salts, can also be used at solar generation plants to allow electric output to match hourly and daily loads.

• *Compressed-air energy storage* uses surplus electricity to compress and store air in airtight, underground reservoirs to be sup-

164

plied to an electricity-generating turbine during peak periods. Now in the demonstration phase, several systems are under construction or operating in different countries, including the United States.

• *Pumped hydro* is used in much the same way as compressed air. Cheap off-peak power is used to pump water to a high-elevation reservoir. When stored power is needed, this water flows back to a lower elevation through a turbine. This technology is fully commercial and provides 17,550 MWe in the United States.

Second, various "balance of system" and other technologies help integrate renewables into existing energy systems:

• *High power semiconductors* convert the relatively low-voltage direct current produced by photovoltaic cells into alternating current so it can enter the grid. Wind generators produce alternating current, but the mechanical governors that regulate their frequency limit power output. All of these connections require high-power semiconductors. Semiconductors made of high-purity silicon are able to handle large voltages and currents without substantial power loss and temperature increases.

• *Transmission technologies* increase the distance over which electricity can be reliably and economically sent, thus making it easier to match renewable energy flows with load centers. While some options are already commercial, other developing technologies include high-power semiconductors, advances in data processing, and superconductivity.

• *Energy-conversion technologies* can be used to produce hydrogen by decomposing water with renewably produced electricity. Hydrogen can then be reconverted to electricity or delivered in pipelines for the same end uses as natural gas. Hydrogen is less expensive to ship long distances than electricity. Hydrogen-combustion technology is in the demonstration stage.

• *Fuel cells* produce electricity by oxidizing a hydrocarbon fuel through an electrochemical reaction that is more efficient and less polluting than combustion. Modular fuel cells may work in conjunction with gasified biomass resources.[54] Phosphoric acid and molten carbonate are among the most promising technologies.

• *Energy-efficiency technologies* complement on-site renewable applications by increasing the ability of electric or thermal renewable applications to serve all remaining building energy needs. Ef-

165

ficiency improvements are occurring in building-construction technology, insulation, advanced glazings, high-efficiency light bulbs, and appliances.

Appendix B: Assumptions and Calculations for Table II-1

For the purposes of this report, the "accessible renewable resource base" is defined as that portion of national renewable energy flows (wind, water, insolation, biomass, and geothermal heat) that can, in principle, be extracted with known conversion technologies that have been demonstrated in the field to produce energy reliably or are projected to become technically viable in the near term. Where data permitted, land available for this resource base was restricted by incompatibility with higher valued uses or legal prohibitions. The base was not constrained, however, by current economic competitiveness, including the ability to match renewable energy flows with various end-use needs occurring in different locations and at different times. Innovations in energy conversion efficiency, storage, and transportation could add to the accessible resource base in the future by allowing lower quality energy flows to be exploited. The ability to compare the size of different renewable resources is limited by qualititative differences in their characteristics and by the uneven quality of the data on which these estimates are based. While not explicitly estimated here, a large band of scientific uncertainty surrounds each of the values shown.

Hydropower	Capacity	Energy	
Conventional capacity	147 Gw	535,000 Gwh	**(1)**
Capacity currently undevelopable by Wild and Scenic Rivers Act (from FERC, 1988)	32.3 Gw	113,000 Gwh	
Ultra low-head and free flow turbines (from SERI, 1990)	17.5 Gw	61,000 Gwh	

Total Capacity   197 Gw   709,000 Gwh

Primary energy conversion factor:
1 Quad/97,000 Gwh   **(2)**

Accessible resource base: **(1)** / **(2)** = 5 Quads/year

Geothermal
    Generating capability is typically estimated on a 30-year basis. To maintain the estimated output on a sustainable basis, the corresponding heat recharge rate is assumed to be twice as long as the period of extraction, 60 years, for a production cycle of 90 years.

Recoverable energy
(based on SERI, 1990, C-2)
    Hydrothermal systems greater or equal to 90 degrees C: 122,000 MW of electricity for 30 years and 285 quads of direct heat
    Geopressurized resources: 160,000 MW of electricity for 30 years (based on 2,000 quads of recoverable energy and the same ratio of recoverable energy to electric capacity as for hydrothermal)
    Hot dry rock: 300,000 MW of electricity for 30 years (based on 6,500 quads of recoverable energy and the same ratio of recoverable energy to electric capacity as for hydrothermal)
    Hydrothermal resources less than 90 degrees C: 80 quads of direct heat
Total electric capacity for 30 years (sum of hydrothermal, geopressurized, and hot dry rock resources): 600,000 MW

Total thermal energy
(sum of thermal energy from hydrothermal
resources above and below 90° C):
                                                   365 quads   **(1)**
Electric output for 30 years at 80%
capacity factor: (based on 600,000
MW capacity) 1.3×10^8 Gwh   **(2)**

Primary energy conversion factor: 1 Quad/97,000 Gwh   **(3)**

167

| Assumed conversion factor for annual sustainable energy production: | 1/90 | **(4)** |

| Sustainable resource base for electricity: | $\dfrac{(2) \times (4)}{(3)}$ = 14 Quads/year |

| Sustainable resource base for thermal energy: | $\overline{(1) \times (4)}$ = 4 Quads/year |

| ***Biomass*** | **Accessible Resource** |

Woody Biomass   10 Quads/year
Other biomass (MSW, recoverable methane,   4 Quads/year
herbaceous crops, other waste materials)
(SERI, 1990, B-4)

Insolation for PV and Thermal Electric
National annual average daily
global solar radiation: 5 kWh/m^2 **(1)**

Primary energy conversion
factor: 1 Quad/97,000 Gwh   **(2)**

Potential land area
(Public and private rangeland,
pasture, and developed): 3×10^{12} m^2 **(3)**
(U.S. Department of Commerce, 1992)

Proportion of potential land area assumed
available for solar energy capture   0.05   **(4)**

Sunlight to electricity conversion factor: 0.15   **(5)**

Allowance for spacing: 0.25   **(6)**
(ground cover ratio based on limiting shading losses
to 5%, from Gordon and Wenger, 1991, p. 125)

Accessible Resource:
$$(1) \times (2) \times (3) \times (4) \times (5) \times (6) = 100 \text{ Quads/year}$$

Wind

Accessible resource estimate: 57 Quads/year
(based on exclusion of all environmentally sensitive land,
all urban land, 50% of forest land, 30% of agricultural land, and
10% of range land; annual wind energy potential from remaining
land in power classes 4–7)
(From Elliott, Wendell, and Gower, 1991, p. 46)

Solar Industrial Process Heat   5 Quads/year
(From Mueller, 1990, p. iv)

Low Temperature Solar Thermal Applications

The resource base for demand side applications is limited by total projected residential and commercial building energy requirements. Renewable energy flows can serve these uses through water heating, space heating and cooling, and daylighting.

Primary energy consumption projections for 2010
(EIA, 1993a, pp. 75-78)

	Primary Energy Consumption (Quads/year)
Residential hot water	3
Residential space heating	5
Residential cooling	2
Commercial space heating	9
Commercial cooling	3
Commercial lighting	5
Total	**27**

The national average solar fraction for residential uses is assumed to be 50% and for commercial uses 25%, yielding 5 Quads/year and 4 Quads/year, respectively.

Total:	9 Quads/year

Ocean Thermal

While the global potential is projected to be about 1,000 Gw, most of this potential is outside of U.S. waters.
Estimated resources that could serve U.S. markets
(U.S. DOE, 1989b, p. 13):   2,000 MW   **(1)**

Assumed capacity factor:	.80	**(2)**
Primary energy conversion factor:	1 Quad/97,000 Gwh	**(3)**

Accessible resource:

24 hrs. x 365 days x **(1)** x **(2)** x **(3)** = 0.1 Quads/year

Notes

1. Within transportation, another 22 quads was used in 1990. Because barriers to the use of renewable energy for transportation are different from those for other applications and because WRI is conducting other studies on transportation energy, the transportation sector is not considered in this report. It does, however, constitute a potentially major market for both renewable electricity and liquid fuels from biomass feedstocks.
2. Not even the current contribution of renewables' to the national energy budget is assured. In California, which by now accounts for about 40 percent of the nation's non-hydro renewable electric capacity, up to 3,000 megawatts of renewable capacity may be financially threatened by falling fossil fuel prices (Smutny-Jones, 1992). At the same time, a large share of the nation's existing private hydro capacity is up for relicensing in the near future, and some will be lost if recent trends hold.
3. One was developed by DOE's Energy Information Administration in conjunction with the National Energy Strategy (EIA, 1990). Another was a collaboration among several federal laboratories (SERI, 1990). The third was developed by a coalition of private nonprofit energy policy organizations (ASE, et al. 1991). A fourth was prepared for the Environmental Protection Agency (Chupka and Howarth, 1992.) These exercises are not entirely independent. Some of their input data are the same, and the assumptions used for base cases are similar. They do, however, vary in their degree of disaggregation, modeling approach, rate of modeled energy demand growth, time period being modeled and, most important, assumptions about alternative scenarios.

4. It should be noted that the structure of the EIA's forecasting model may make long-run results somewhat insensitive to conventional macroeconomic variables.

5. In addition, recovery of methane from landfills and other anaerobic sources for energy reduces release of this gas into the atmosphere, while the use of passive solar cooling reduces the need for ozone-depleting refrigerants.

6. Accordingly, facilities that manufacture renewable energy equipment represent an investment in reducing emissions that is paid back in about as much time as it takes the facility to become a net energy producer. As a caveat, any increase in the use of fossil-based "spinning reserves" (operating units that are not connected to the grid unless needed to meet demand when intermittent renewable generation is low) would offset some carbon savings. Any increase in the use of fossil-based spinning reserves (operating units that are not connected to the grid unless needed to meet unexpected demand) would also reduce net carbon savings (Chupka and Howarth, 1992).

7. GDP is the value of final goods produced within the country.

8. Global 2100 is a "top-down" model for analyzing the costs of mitigating warming; it does not model the effects of individual renewable or energy efficiency technologies.

9. The future of nuclear power is subject to many factors whose analysis is beyond the scope of this report.

10. As with climate risks, renewables' other environmental benefits may be time-dependent. For example, since some terrestrial and aquatic ecosystem effects from acid rain are not reversible, the sooner that emissions of acid rain precursors are reduced, the greater the benefits.

11. Renewably generated electricity could also substitute for petroleum use in transportation. Other renewables not directly considered in this report could play an even larger role.

12. The percentage of total life cycle costs comprised of fuel costs determines the economic benefits retained within the region (New York State Energy Office, 1992).

13. Solar water heating and passive space heating were the only renewable technologies in the solar scenario.

14. Technological changes in both renewable and nonrenewable energy industries could affect employment creation. From 1980 to 1991, both total national employment and labor intensity (employees per quad) in fossil fuels have generally declined. In fact, coal production has gone from 13,000 employees per quad in 1980 to 6,000 in 1991 (ASE, AGA, SEIA, 1992). Technological change in renewable energy production could also reduce labor intensity.

15. The Btu content of oil was proposed to be taxed at a higher rate than other fuels.

16. Another concern with energy taxes is that they are viewed as falling most heavily on lower income groups. Energy tax strategies can be designed to mitigate this concern without losing the economic benefits of a tax-based policy. Further, it is becoming more and more clear that a significant fraction of the existing burden of pollution falls on these same groups. They are likely, therefore, to also benefit from such tax programs.

17. This preference has been demonstrated by ratepayer surveys of willingness to pay for clean electric generation technologies that have now been conducted by several utilities (*See*, for example, Buchanan, 1991).

18. Along with CO_2 regulations, future SO_x regulations will probably be tightened at the state or regional levels. NO_x control may also be necessary to reduce ground-level ozone.

19. In other jurisdictions, utilities are acting on their own to reduce such risks. Several utilities have pledged to reduce their greenhouse gas emissions. Bonneville Power Administration currently rules out coal generation as a possible resource acquisition and requires fossil fuel developers to provide evidence that they could absorb carbon-reduction compliance costs. The New England Electric System incorporates environmental externalities in its resource plan by specifying pollution offsets and acquisitions of renewables (Hachey and Makowka, 1992).

20. By comparison, the total value of energy production in 1990 was about $475 billion.

21. The estimates for wind and geothermal subsidies were made using the same 1989 high-subsidy estimate approach as those

for the nonrenewable energy sources in the Koplow study: 1989 kWh generation.

22. New tax subsidies for renewables may be justified when targeted to specific commercialization barriers. *(See Chapter VI.)*

23. For example, the tax liability of the gas industry is influenced by several characteristics not shared by the solar industry: (1) drilling costs constitute a major expenditure in gas exploration and development, (2) exploration is inherently risky, and (3) the industry is extracting a depletable asset.

24. Many recommendations in this chapter draw heavily from a commissioned paper by David Moskovitz: "Renewable Energy: Barriers and Opportunities; Walls and Bridges."

25. Integrated resource planning is a more recent term for "least cost planning" and one that explicitly takes account of demand- and supply-side acquisitions, social costs, and risks associated with resource options, as well as the need for public participation (Hirst, 1992a).

26. These states are California, Maine, Florida, Georgia, New York, Alabama, Michigan, North Carolina, Virginia, Massachusetts.

27. During a generating unit's lifetime, a utility incurs pre-construction costs (such as engineering and feasibility studies), capital costs, fuel and operating costs, and, finally, decommissioning costs. The farther in the future that these costs come due, the harder they are to predict accurately.

28. Solar and wind-based generating equipment also has relatively high salvage value; should forecasted demand diverge greatly from actual demand, owners can recoup some losses.

29. Of course, renewable developers want to maximize plant operation to recover their fixed costs, regardless of utility needs.

30. Capacity factor is the ratio of annual kWh output to potential kWh output based on the nameplate capacity rating of the unit.

31. Because avoided cost is determined by peak demand, the times in which an intermittent resource has greatest value to the utility need not coincide with times of the resource's highest power output (Rahman, 1989).

32. When instantaneous capacity exceeds system demand, renewable generators can be operated at partial load, by, for instance, feathering the blades on wind turbines. Because of their low

operating costs, however, it may be more economical to take full advantage of the energy they provide to the extent that nonrenewable generators can be run economically at partial loads (Grubb, 1991).

33. This discussion focuses on bulk power applications of renewables (generally still smaller than central station fossil/nuclear generation). Distributed applications tend to be easier to integrate into existing utility infrastructure.

34. Transmission access is a function of adequate capacity, acceptable price, and reasonable terms of service.

35. Technologies include flat-plate collectors for low-temperature preheating applications, parabolic troughs for intermediate process steam and direct heat, and parabolic dish technologies for high temperature direct heat.

36. These may arise from uncertainty over a technology's lifetime performance, energy consumption in the absence of the renewable application, or future fuel prices.

37. As discussed in Chapter VI, a policy tool's cost-effectiveness is enhanced if it increases market demand sufficiently and for long enough for cost reductions to be achieved.

38. Buildings constructed in the next few years will last well into the next century, when tightening environmental constraints on coal use could drive natural gas prices even higher.

39. While there is some evidence that housing markets do capitalize part of the value of energy investment, the period of ownership still affects rates of return (Laquatra, 1987).

40. The challenge of crafting cost-effective incentives is discussed further in Chapter VI.

41. At the federal level, the Energy Policy Act of 1992 begins to address these issues by making energy costs and investments separate line items in federal department budgets.

42. For summer peak loads, passive design can also reduce air conditioning and ventilation requirements.

43. Of course, any inequities resulting from DSM-driven rate increases must be viewed from the perspective that rate increases also result from inefficient energy use.

44. Nonetheless, price regulatory and other policy reforms do tend to make commercialization investments more attractive.

175

45. For example, the cost of electricity from PV installations is affected by improvements in light-to-electricity conversion efficiency, mass production, manufacturing procedures, and balance-of-system costs (Weissman, 1992). While accumulated experience is responsible for much of the cost reduction in wind energy during the 1980s, wind turbines have been enlarged (> 250 kw) to capture more wind energy and save on operation and maintenance costs. At the same time, however, transmissions and generators are mass produced only for machines up to 250 kw, limiting the cost advantage associated with further increases in turbine size (*Wind Energy Weekly*, 3-9-92). For applications in the building sector, costs reflect not only manufacturing economies, but also marketing and installation costs. Passive solar energy costs are considered particularly sensitive to design and construction experience.

46. The large fixed costs of entering renewable energy equipment manufacturing—namely, those of R&D and specialized capital equipment—limits the total number of firms pursuing each renewable technology. Early entrants have the best chance of capturing market share. For renewable energy equipment that is internationally traded, the economic benefits of getting to the market early may be large enough to allow specific companies or nations to garner major shares of world markets. If early advantage temporarily forecloses further market entry, these producers or countries could collect unusually high returns on investment, though precedents are few (Ford and Suyker, 1990).

47. Renewable R&D funding in Europe was much more stable between 1980 and 1989 (Janssen, 1991).

48. The federal government is still funding other energy technologies with long-term uncertain payoffs (notably nuclear fusion).

49. For a general discussion of institutional models for public RD&D that exist either in the United States or elsewhere, *see* Heaton, Repetto, and Sobin, 1992.

50. Thus, for example, if the government expected a one-third success rate for projects, it would seek a threefold return on its subsidy through royalty payments for successful projects.

51. The four projects were a 30 MW wind project, production of solar parabolic troughs, a one MW PV demonstration, and a

100 MW central receiver power plant.

52. The performance and cost of renewable energy technologies has been improving rapidly. *See,* for example, Johansson et al., 1992 and Larson et al., 1992.

53. Pumped hydro is often included as well; here, it is treated as a storage technology.

54. Improved gasification technologies, more efficient than direct combustion, would facilitate applications of biomass resources. Gasified biomass could then be used as a feedstock for fuel cells or advanced turbines.

REFERENCES

Advisory Committee on Renewable Energy and Energy Efficiency Joint Ventures. 1992. *Report to the Secretary of Energy: Recommendations for Implementation of Public Law 101-218 Joint Ventures.* Washington, DC.

Aitken, Donald W. 1992. "Impact of Sustained Orderly Development on Costs of Renewable Electric Energy Technologies for the California Energy Commission." Submitted by Coalition for Energy Efficiency and Renewable Technologies, Sacramento, CA.

Aitken, Donald W. and P. Bony. 1993. "Passive Solar Production Housing and the Utilities," *Solar Today.* Boulder, CO. March/April. Vol. 7, No. 2, pp. 23–26.

Alliance to Save Energy (ASE), American Gas Association (AGA), Solar Energy Industries Association (SEIA). 1992. *An Alternative Energy Future.* Washington, D.C., April.

Alliance to Save Energy, American Council for an Energy Efficient Economy (ACEEE), National Resources Defense Council (NRDC), Union of Concerned Scientists (UCS), 1991. *America's Energy Choices: Investing in a Strong Economy and Clean Environment.* Union of Concerned Scientists: Cambridge, MA.

American Wind Energy Association (AWEA). 1992. "PURPA Handbook for Independent Electric Power Producers." Washington, DC.

___. 1991. "Wind Energy—A Resource for the 1990s and Beyond." Washington, DC.

Anderjko, Dennis A. 1991. *Assessment of Solar Energy Technologies.* American Solar Energy Society. Boulder, CO.

Anderson, Dennis. 1992. *The Energy Industry and Global Warming: New Roles for International Aid.* Overseas Development Institute, London.

Association of State Energy Research and Technology Transfer Institutions (ASERTTI). 1992. Personal Communication. New York City.

Awerbuch, Shimon. 1993. "The Surprising Role of Risk in Utility Integrated Resource Planning." *The Electricity Journal,* Volume 6, Number 3.

___. 1992. "Measuring the Costs of Photovoltaics in an IRP Framework," *Proceedings of the Fourth National Conference on Integrated Resource Planning.* Washington, DC. February.

Baily, Martin Neil and Ashok K. Chakrabarti. 1985. "Innovation and U.S. Competitiveness." *The Brookings Review,* Fall.

Bain, Don. 1992a. *Wind/Solar: A Regulatory Guide to Leasing, Permitting, and Licensing in Idaho, Montana, Oregon, and Washington.* Bonneville Power Administration. Portland, OR.

___. 1992b. "Wind Power Sales and Siting Issues" Windpower' 92. Seattle, WA.

Bennington, G. 1979. *Toward a National Plan for the Accelerated Commercialization of Solar Energy.* Prepared for U.S. Department of Energy.

Birk, James R. 1992. "Enlightened and Endless Electricity." *EPRI Journal,* Vol. 17, No. 8. p. 1.

Bohi, D. R. and M.A. Toman. 1992. *Energy Security Externalities and Policies.* Resources for the Future, Washington, DC. May.

Brower, Michael C., Michael W. Tennis, Eric W. Denzler, Mark M. Kaplan. 1993. *Powering the Midwest: Renewable Electricity for the Economy and the Environment.* Union of Concerned Scientists, Cambridge, MA.

Brown, Marylin A. and C. Robert Wilson. 1992. "Promoting the Commercialization of Energy Innovations: An Evaluation of the Energy-Related Inventions Program" *Policy Studies Journal,* Vol. 20, No. 1.

Buchanan, Shepard. 1991. "Contingent Valuation Study of the Environmental Costs of Electricity Generating Technologies." in *Environmental Costs of Electric Power,* ed. by Olav Hohmeyer and Richard Ottinger. Springer-Verlag, New York, pp. 159–67.

Burtraw, Dallas and Alan J. Krupnick. 1992. *The Social Costs of Electricity: How Much of the Camel to Let into the Tent?* (Discussion Paper QE92-15.) Resources for the Future: Washington, DC. April.

Byrne, John, Constantine Hadjilambrinos and Young-Doo Wang. 1992a. "The Role of PV in Demand-Side Management: Policy and Industry Challenges." In *Proceedings of the 11th Photovoltaic Advanced Research and Development Project Review Meeting* (forthcoming).

Byrne, John, Young-Doo Wang and Steven M. Hoffman. 1992b. *Utility and Commission Attitudes Towards Photovoltaic Technology and Demand-Side Management in the Utility Sector.* Newark, DE: Center for Energy and Urban Policy Research, College of Urban Affairs and Public Policy, University of Delaware.

Cadogan, John B., Kathryn E. George, Thomas C. Schweizer, and Joseph M. Cohen. 1992. "The Risks of Conventional Utility Supply Sources and the Rewards of Renewable Energy." Presented at Windpower '92, Seattle, WA.

California Energy Commission (CEC). 1992. *Energy Technology Status Report.* Sacramento, November.

___. 1991. *Energy Technology Status Report: Final Report.* Sacramento.

Carlsmith, Roger, W. McMahon and D. Santino. 1990. "Energy Efficiency: How Far Can We Go?" ORNL, TM-11441. Oak Ridge National Laboratory. Oak Ridge, TN. January.

Chupka, Marc and David Howarth. 1992. *Renewable Electric Generation: An Assessment of Air Pollution Prevention Potential.* EPA/400/R-92/005. Washington, DC: ICF Inc. for EPA. March.

City of Houston, 1989. *The Impact of Budgetary Incentives on Energy Management.* Urban Consortium Energy Task Force, Houston, TX.

City of Seattle, 1988. *Integrating Energy Efficiency Into Municipal Purchasing Decisions: Defining the Framework.* Urban Consortium Energy Task Force, Seattle, WA.

Clemmer, Steve. 1993. *Economic Impacts of Renewable Energy Use in Wisconsin.* Wisconsin Department of Administration, Division of Energy and Intergovernmental Relations. Madison, WI.

Cleveland, Cutler J. 1992. "Energy Quality and Energy Surplus in the Extraction of Fossil Fuels in the U.S." *Ecological Economics.* Vol. 6, No. 2, pp. 139–162. Amsterdam. October.

Cline, William. 1992a. *Global Warming: The Economic Stakes*. Institute for International Economics, Washington, DC. May.

___. 1992b. "Energy Efficiency and Greenhouse Abatement Costs (Comment on Lovins and Lovins)," *Climatic Change,* Volume 22: pp. 95–97.

Cohen, Linda R. and Roger G. Noll, 1991. *The Technology Pork Barrel*. The Brookings Institution, Washington, DC.

Cohen, S.D., J.H. Eto, C.A. Goldman, J. Beldock, and G. Crandall. 1990. " A Survey of State PUC Activities to Incorporate Environmental Externalities into Electric Utility Planning and Regulation." National Association of Regulatory Utility Commissioners. Washington, DC. May.

Collins, Sally D. 1990. "Newberry National Volcanic Monument: Making a Consensus Process Work." USDA Forest Service, Bend, OR.

Committee on Assessment of Research Needs for Wind Turbine Rotor Materials Technology, et al. 1991. *Assessment of Research Needs for Wind Turbine Rotor Materials Technology*. National Research Council, National Academy Press, Washington, DC.

Cook, James H., J. Beyea, and K.H. Keeler. 1991. "Potential Impacts of Biomass Production in the United States on Biological Diversity," *Annual Review of Energy*. Washington, DC.

Council on Economic Priorities. 1979. *Jobs and Energy: The Employment and Economic Impacts of Nuclear Power, Conservation, and Other Energy Options*. New York, NY.

Crousillant, Enrique and Spiros Martzoukos. 1991. *Decision Making Under Uncertainty: An Option Valuation Approach to Power Planning*. World Bank Industry and Energy Department Working Paper, Energy Series Paper No. 39, Washington, DC. August.

Dasgupta, Partha and Geoffrey Heal. 1981. *Economic Theory and Exhaustible Resources*. Cambridge University Press, Great Britain.

Dennis, Michael L., E. Jonathan Soderstrom, Walter S. Koncinski, Jr. and Betty Cavanaugh. 1990. "Effective Dissemination of Energy-Related Information." *American Psychologist*, Vol. 45, No. 10: pp. 1109–1117.

Douglas, John. 1991. "Fuel Cells for Urban Power." *EPRI Journal*. Vol. 16, No. 6, pp. 4–11.

Dower, Roger and Mary Beth Zimmerman. 1992. *The Right Climate for Carbon Taxes: Creating Economic Incentives to Protect the Atmosphere.* World Resources Institute, Washington, DC.

Dowlatabadi, Hadi and Micheal Toman. 1991. *Technology Options for Electricity Generation.* Resources for the Future, Washington, DC.

Dubin, J. A. and S.E. Henson. 1988. "The Distributional Effects of the Federal Energy Tax Act." *Resources and Energy*, 10: 191–212.

Eaton, Michael. California Chapter, Sierra Club. Personal Communication, 1991.

Elliot, D.L., L.L. Wendell, and G.L. Gower. 1991. "U.S. Areal Wind Resource Estimates Considering Environmental and Land-Use Exclusions." Battelle Pacific Northwest Laboratory, Richland, WA. September.

Energy Daily. December 3, 1991.

Energy Information Administration (EIA). 1993a. "Annual Energy Outlook 1993 with Projections to 2010." U.S. Department of Energy DOE/EIA-0383(93). Washington, DC. January.

___. 1993b. *Annual Energy Review, 1992.* Washington, DC.

___. 1992a. "EIA Survey." *The Solar Letter*, 12-25-93.

___. 1992b. *Assumptions for the Annual Energy Outlook 1992.* Washington, DC. January.

___. 1992c. *Estimates of U.S. Biofuels Consumption 1990.* U.S. Department of Energy, Washington, DC. October.

___. 1992d. *Federal Energy Subsidies: Direct and Indirect Interventions in Energy Markets.* Washington, DC.

___. 1992e. *Solar Collector Manufacturing Activity, 1990.* DOE/EIA-0174(90). Washington, DC. February.

___. 1991. *Geothermal Energy in the Western United States and Hawaii: Resources and Projected Electricity Generation Supplies.* DOE/EIA-0544, Washington, DC. September.

___. 1990. *Renewable Energy Excursion: Supporting Analysis for the National Energy Strategy.* Washington, DC. December.

Farhar-Pilgrim, Barbara and Charles T. Unseld. 1985. *America's Solar Potential.* Praeger Special Studies, Praeger Scientific, Westport, CT.

Federal Energy Regulatory Commission, (FERC). 1992. *Annual Qualifying Facilities Report: Fiscal Year 1980 Through Fiscal Year 1992.* Washington, DC.

183

___. 1988. *Hydroelectric Power Resources of the United States,* FERC-0070, Washington, DC. January.

Fenn, Scott. 1989. *Power Plays.* Investor's Responsibility Research Center, Washington, DC.

Fenn, Scott and Susan Williams. 1991. *A White Paper on Renewable Energy Financing Barriers and Constraints.* Investor Responsibility Research Center, Washington, DC. November.

Ferry, Steven. 1990. *Law of Independent Power,* Clark Boardman Pub., N.Y., NY.

Florida Solar Energy Center (FSEC). 1990. *1990 Annual Report.* Cape Canaveral, FL.

Ford, Robert and Wim Suyker. 1990. "Industrial Subsidies in the OECD Economies." *OECD Economic Studies,* No. 15. Paris.

Frankel, Eugene. 1986. "Technology, Politics and Ideology: The Vicissitudes of Federal Solar Energy Policy, 1974–1983." *The Politics of Energy Research and Development, Volume 3,* ed. by John Byrne and Daniel Rich. Transaction Books, New Brunswick, NJ., pp. 61–88.

Geller, Howard, John DeCicco, and Skip Laitner. 1992. *Energy Efficiency and Job Creation: The Employment and Income Benefits from Investing in Energy Conserving Technologies.* American Council for an Energy-Efficient Economy, Washington, DC.

Gilinsky, Victor and I.C. Bupp. 1992. "Premature Nuclear Plant Closings." Cambridge Energy Research Associates. Decision Brief. Cambridge, MA.

Givoni, B. 1991. "Characteristics, Design Implications and Applicability of Passive Solar Heating Systems for Building." *Solar Energy.* 47(6): 425–36.

Gordon, J.M. and H.J. Wenger. 1991. "On Optimizing Central-Station Photovoltaic Solar Power Systems: The Role of Field Layout, Shading, Tracking and Array Geometry." *1991 Solar World Congress, Volume 1, Part 1.* pp. 125–130.

Green, Christopher. 1992. "Economics and the Greenhouse Effect." *Climatic Change,* Volume 22: pp. 265–291.

Grubb, M.J. 1991. "The Integration of Renewable Electricity Sources." *Energy Policy,* Vol. 19, No. 7.: pp. 670–688.

Gupta, B.P. 1991. "Solar Thermal Technology—Is it Ready for the Market?" National Renewable Energy Laboratory, Golden, CO. December.

Hachey, Michael and Stephen D. Makowka. 1992. "The NEP Renewable Energy Initiative: Objectives and Experiences" *Proceedings—Fourth National Conference on Integrated Resource Planning: Burlington, Vermont; September 13–16, 1992.* National Association of Regulatory Utility Commissioners: Washington, DC. September.

Hall, Charles A.S. and Cutler J. Cleveland. 1981. "Petroleum Drilling and Production in the United States: Yield per Effort and Net Energy Analysis." *Science.* 211:576–579.

Hamrin, Jan. 1992a. "Renewable Resource Policies on the State Level" *Proceedings-Fourth National Conference on Integrated Resource Planning: Burlington, Vermont; September 13–16.* National Association of Regulatory Utility Commissioners: Washington, DC. September.

Hamrin, Jan. 1992b. Personal Communication.

Hamrin, Jan and Nancy Rader. 1993. *Investing in the Future: A Regulator's Guide to Renewables.* The National Association of Regulatory Utility Commissioners. Washington, DC.

Hasset, Kevin A. and Gilbert E, Metcalf. 1993. "Energy Conservation Investment: Do Consumers Discount the Future Correctly?" *Energy Policy*, Vol. 21, No. 6, pp. 710–716. Oxford, UK. June.

___. 1992. *Energy Tax Credits and Residential Conservation Investment.* Columbia University, New York. February.

Heaton, George R., Robert Repetto, and Rodney Sobin. 1992. *Backs to the Future: U.S. Government Policy Toward Environmentally Critical Technology.* World Resources Institute, Washington, DC.

Hirst, Eric. 1992a. *A Good Integrated Resource Plan: Guidelines for Electric Utilities and Regulators.* Oak Ridge National Laboratory, ORNL/CON-354, Oak Ridge, TN.

___. 1992b. *Effects of Utility DSM Programs on Risk.* ORNL/CON-346. Oak Ridge National Laboratory, Oak Ridge, TN.

Hirst, Eric, Richard Goeltz, Mark Thornsjo, and Debra Sundin. 1983. *Evaluation of Home Energy Audit and Retrofit Loan Programs in Minnesota: the Northern States Power Experience.* Oak Ridge National Laboratory, Oak Ridge, TN.

Hohmeyer, Olav. 1992a. "Renewables and the Full Costs of Energy." *Energy Policy*, Volume 20, No. 4., pp. 365–375.

___. 1992b. "The Social Costs of Electricity Generation: Wind and Photovoltaic vs. Fossil and Nuclear Energy." *Energy and Environment: The Policy Challenge, Volume 6*. Transaction Publishers, New Brunswick, CT.

Holdren, John P. 1980. "Renewables in the U.S. Energy Future: How Much, How Fast"? Invited Paper for the National Conference on Renewable Energy Technologies, Honolulu. Energy and Resources Group Working Paper ERG WP-80-13, University of California, Berkeley. *Energy—The International Journal*, Vol. 6, No. 9, pp. 901–916, September.

International Energy Agency. 1987. *Renewable Sources of Energy*. OECD, Paris, France.

Interstate Solar Cordination Council. 1991. "Networking: Renewable Energy in the States, 1991 Directory." ISCC, Austin, TX.

Jackson, Tim. 1991. "Least-Cost Greenhouse Planning: Supply Curves for Global Warming Abatement." *Energy Policy*, Volume 19, No. 1, pp. 35–46.

Janssen, Rodney. 1991. *Report on Renewable Energy Policies in Western Europe*. Energy, Mines and Resources Canada, Ottawa, Ontario.

Johansson, Thomas B., Henry Kelly, Amulya D. N. Reddy, and Robert H. Williams. 1992. *Renewables Energy: Sources for Fuels and Electricity*. Island Press, Washington, DC.

Johnson, Stephen B., 1979. "A Survey of State Approaches to Solar Energy Incentives." Solar Energy Research Institute, Golden CO.

Kahn, Robert D. 1992. "Power Plant Siting and Public Acceptance." Washington, State Energy Strategy Committee, Seattle, WA.

Kaminow, Ira P. 1989. *Current Subsidy Estimates of Selected U.S. Production Subsidies*. Hill and Knowlton, Inc., Washington, DC.

Katzev, Richard D., and Theodore Johnson. 1987. *Promoting Energy Conservation*. Westview Press, Boulder, CO.

Kaufman, Robert J. and Cleveland, Cutler J. 1991. "Policies to Increase U.S. Oil Production: Likely to Fail, Damage the Economy, and Damage the Environment." *Annual Review of Energy and the Environment*, Volume 16. Palo Alto, CA. pp. 379–400.

Kelly, Henry. 1992. "Federal Demonstration Programs," *National Solar Energy Conference*, Cocoa Beach, FL., June 13–18.

Kelly, Henry, Carl Weinberg and Robert Williams. 1992. "Renewable Energy Policy Initiatives to Improve the Productivity and

Competitiveness of the U.S. Economy and Meet the Environmental Challenges of the 21st Century." Unpublished Draft.

Kline, Stephen Jay. 1990. "Innovation Styles in Japan and the United States: Cultural Bases; Implications for Competitiveness," *The 1989 Thurston Lecture*. Stanford University, Stanford.

Koplow, Douglas. 1993. *Federal Energy Subsidies: Energy, Environmental and Fiscal Impacts*. Alliance to Save Energy, Washington, DC.

Krause, Florentin, John Busch, and Jon Kooney. 1992. "Incorporating Global Warming Risks in Power Sector Planning: A Case Study of the New England Region." Lawrence Berkeley Laboratory. Meeting of National Association of Regulatory Utility Commissioners. Washington, DC. March.

Krause, Florentine and Joseph Eto. 1988. *Least-Cost Utility Planning, Volume 2: The Demand Side: Conceptual and Methodological Issues*. National Association of Regulatory Utility Commissioners, Washington, DC. December.

Kreith, Frank, Paul Norton, and Thomas Lang. 1991. "The Potential of Solar, Renewable, and Energy Conservation Systems to Reduce Global Warming." Boulder, CO.

Krupnick, Alan J. 1993. "Benefit Transfers and Valuation of Environmental Improvements." *Resources*. Resources for the Future. No. 110, Winter.

Laitner, Skip. 1993. "Energy Savings and Job Impacts from the Proposed Energy Tax." Washington, DC.

Lamarre, Leslie. 1992. "A Growth Market in Wind Power." *EPRI Journal*, Vol. 17, No. 8: pp. 4–15.

___. 1991. "Shaping DSM as a Resource." *EPRI Journal*, Vol. 16, No. 7: pp. 5–15.

Laquatra, Joseph. 1987. "Valuation of Household Investment Energy-Efficient Design." *Energy Efficiency: Perspectives on Individual Behavior*. Cornell University, Ithaca, NY.

Larson, Ronal W., Frank Vignola, and Ron West. 1992. *Economics of Solar Energy Technologies*. American Solar Energy Society. Boulder, CO.

Lashof, Daniel A. and Dennis A. Tirpak, eds. 1990. *Policy Options for Stabilizing Global Climate, Report to Congress: Executive Summary*. U.S. Environmental Protection Agency, Washington, DC.

Lind, Robert C., Kenneth J. Arrow, Gordon R. Corey, et al. 1982. *Discounting for Time and Risk in Energy Policy*. Resources for the Future, Washington, DC.

Lotker, Michael. 1991. *Barriers to Commercialization of Large-Scale Solar Electricity: Lessons Learned from the LUZ Experience*. Sandia National Laboratories, Oak Ridge, TN.

Manne, Alan S. and Richard Richels. 1992. *Buying Greenhouse Insurance: The Economic Costs of CO_2 Emission Limits*. MIT Press, Cambridge, MA.

Marchetti, C. and N. Nakicenovic. 1979. *The Dynamics of Energy Systems and the Logistic Substitution Model*. International Institute for Applied Systems Analysis, Laxenburg, Austria.

Masters, C.D., D. H. Root, and E.D. Attanasi. 1991. "Resource Constraints in Petroleum Production Potential," *Science*, Vol. 253, No. 5016.

___. 1990. "World Oil and Gas Resources—Future Production Realities." *Annual Review of Energy*, Volume 15. Palo Alto, CA., pp. 23–52.

Maycock, Paul D. 1993. *PV News*. Vol. 12, No. 2., February.

___. 1992. "Photovoltaics as a Customer Peaking and Demand Management Option." PV Energy Systems, Casanova, VA.

McCormack, Katie. Pacific Gas and Electric Research Department, San Ramon, CA. Personal Communication, 1993.

McGowan, Francis. 1991. "Controlling the Greenhouse Effect: The Role of Renewables." *Energy Policy*, March 1991, pp. 110–118.

Meade, William R. and David F. Teitelbaum. 1989. "A Guide to Renewable Energy and Least Cost Utility Planning." Interstate Solar Coordination Council, St. Paul, MN.

Meridian Corporation. 1989. *Energy System Emissions and Materiel Requirements*. Alexandria, VA.

Mills, David and Bill Keepin. 1993. "Baseload Solar Power: Near-Term Prospects for Load Following Solar Thermal Electricity." *Energy Policy*. Volume 21, No. 8. August.

Moore, Taylor. 1992. "Natural Gas for Utility Generation," *Electric Power Research Institute Journal*. pp. 4–15. Palo Alto, CA. January/February.

Moskovitz, David. 1992. "Renewable Energy: Barriers and Opportunities, Walls, and Bridges." Background paper for the World Resources Institute. Gardiner, ME.

Mueller, E.A. 1990. "Estimating the Potential for Solar Thermal Applications in the Industrial Process Heat Market, 1990–2030." U.S. Department of Energy, Office of Conservation and Renewable Energy. Washington, DC.

Muller, Frank, Skip Laitner, Alan Miller, and Lyuba Zarsky. 1992. "Jobs Benefits of Expanding Investment in Solar Energy." *Solar Industry Journal.* Fourth Quarter, pp.17–25.

Murley, Clifford, Donald Osborn, and P. Ross Gorman. 1993. "SMUD's Solar Domestic Hot Water Incentive Program." Proceedings from ASES Solar '93 Conference, Washington, DC.

Musgrave, Richard and Peggy Musgrave. 1989. *Public Finance in Theory and Practice.* McGraw Hill, New York.

National Appropriate Technology Assistance Service (NATAS). 1992. "Tax Credits and Incentives." U.S. Department of Energy. Butte, MT. March.

National Association of State Energy Officials. 1991. *Renewable Energy Survey.* Washington, DC.

National Renewable Energy Laboratory (NREL). 1992. *A National Program for Energy-Efficient Mortgages and Home Energy Rating Systems: A Blueprint for Action.* Washington, DC.

New Energy and Industrial Technology Development Organization (NEDO). 1991. *1990 Annual Report.* Tokyo.

New York State Energy Office. 1992. *Hydro-Quebec Economic Study: Draft Appendices.* Albany, NY.

Nordhaus, W.D. 1991. "Economic Approaches to Greenhouse Warming," in *Global Warming: Economic Policy Responses.* Dornbusch and Porterba, eds. MIT Press, Cambridge, MA.

___. 1973. "The Allocation of Energy Resources." *Brookings Papers* 3:529–70.

Nordmann, Thomas, Luzi Clavedetscher, and Raimund Hachler. 1991. "100 KW Grid-Connected PV Installation Along Motorway and Railway." *Solar World Congress*, Volume I, Part I. Pergamon Press, Oxford. pp. 131–136.

Norgaard, Richard B. 1991. "Economic Indicators of Resource Scarcity: A More Critical Reply," *Journal of Environmental Economics and Management*, Volume 21, No. 2. September.

___. 1990. "Economic Indicators of Resource Scarcity: A Critical Essay." *Journal of Environmental Economics and Management.*

Volume 19, No. 1, July, pp. 19–25.

North American Electric Reliability Council (NERC). 1993. *Electricity Supply and Demand, 1993–2002*. Princeton, NJ. June.

___. 1991. *Electricity Supply and Demand, 1991–2000*. Princeton, NJ. June.

Oak Ridge National Laboratory (ORNL). 1989. *Energy Technology R&D: What Could Make A Difference*, Vol. 2, Part 3. Oak Ridge National Laboratory, Oak Ridge, TN.

Oak Ridge National Laboratory (ORNL) and Resources for the Future. 1992. *U.S.–EC Fuel Cycle Study: Background Document to the Approach and Issues*. Oak Ridge National Laboratory, Oak Ridge, TN.

Oberg, Kenneth. 1992. "The Impact of Production Incentives on Financing Wind Energy Projects," Windpower '92. Seattle, WA.

O'Driscoll, Mary. 1992. "Ohio PUC Proposes Competitive Bidding, Open Access Rules." *The Energy Daily*, Vol. 20, No. 245: pp. 1–2.

Office of Technology Assessment. 1992. *Building Energy Efficiency*. OTA-E-518. Washington, DC: U.S. Government Printing Office.

___. 1991. *Energy Technology Choices: Shaping Our Future*. Washington, DC. July.

___. 1985. *New Electric Power Technologies: Problems and Prospects for the 1990's*. Washington, DC.

Olson, Mancur. 1965. *The Logic of Collective Action*. Harvard University Press, Cambridge, MA.

Organisation for Economic Co-operation and Development (OECD). 1988. *Environmental Impacts of Renewable Energy: The OECD Compass Project*. Paris, France.

Ottinger, Richard L., David R. Nooley, Nicholas A. Robinson, David R. Holas, and Susan E. Babb. 1990. *Environmental Costs of Electricity*. Pace University Center for Environmental Legal Studies, White Plains, NY.

Palmer, Karen L. and Alan Krupnick. 1991. "Environmental Costing and Electric Utilities' Planning and Investment." Resources for the Future, Fall 1991, No. 105. Washington, DC.

Palmer, Karen, Peter Fox-Penner, David Simpson, Michael Toman, Gayle Killam. 1992. *Contracting Incentives in Electricity Generation Fuel Markets*, Discussion Paper 92-07. Resources for the Future, Energy and Natural Resources Division, Washington, DC. February.

Parody, Alan. Advanced Photovoltaics Systems. Personal Communication, 1992.

Peelle, Elizabeth. 1988. "Beyond the Nimby Impasse II: Public Participation in an Age of Distrust." Oak Ridge National Laboratory, Oak Ridge, TN.

PV News. 1992.

Rader, Nancy. 1989. *Power Surge: The Status and Near-Term Potential of Renewable Energy Technologies.* Public Citizen. Washington, DC. May.

Rader, Nancy, Ken Bossong, Jonathan Becker, Daniel Borson, and Cleo Manuel. 1990. *The Power of the States: A Fifty-State Survey of Renewable Energy.* Public Citizen. Washington, DC. June.

Rahman, Salfur. 1989. "Economic Impact of Integrating Photovoltaics with Conventional Electric Utility Operation." 89 SM 621-4 EC. Blacksburg, VA: Virginia Polytechnic Institute and State University.

Rastler, Daniel. 1992 "Distributed Generation." *EPRI Journal,* Vol. 17, No. 3.: pp. 28–30.

Reid, Michael W. 1992. *Incentives for Demand-Side Management.* National Association of Regulatory Utility Commissioners, Washington, DC. January.

Renewable Energy Institute (REI). 1986. *Annual Renewable Energy Technology Review: Progress Through 1984.* Washington, DC.

Rezendez, Victor. 1992. *Energy R&D: DOE's Prioritization and Budgeting Process for Renewable Energy Research.* U.S. General Accounting Office, Washington, DC.

Rich, Daniel and David J. Roessner. 1990. "Tax Credits and US Solar Commercialization Policy," *Energy Policy,* Volume 18, Issue 2, pp. 186–198.

Roessner, J.D. 1980. *Making Solar Laws Work: A Study of State Solar Energy Incentives—Volume 1: Executive Summary."* Solar Energy Research Institute, Golden, CO. November.

Rose, Adam, Ben Nakayama, and Brandt Stevens. 1982. "Modern Energy Region Development and Income Distribution: An Input-Output Analysis," *Journal of Environmental Economics and Management.* Vol. 9, pp. 149–64.

Sachs, Harvey M., Frank Muller and Alan S. Miller. 1993. "A Strategy for More Rapid Expansion of the Grid-Connected Photovoltaic Market." *Solar '93; Technical Paper; Proceedings of the 1993 Annual Conference.* American Solar Energy Society. pp. 158–164.

San Martin, Robert L. 1989. *Environmental Emissions from Energy Technology Systems: The Total Fuel Cycle.* U.S. Department of Energy, Washington, DC.

Saunders, Harry D. 1992. "The Khazzoom-Brookes Postulate and Neoclassical Growth." *The Energy Journal*, Volume 13, No. 4. pp. 130–148.

Sawyer, Stephen W. 1986. *Renewable Energy, Progress, Prospects.* Association of American Geographers: Washington, DC.

Sawyer, Stephen, W. and Richard R. Lancaster. 1985. "Renewable Energy Tax Incentives: Status, Evaluation Attempts, Continuing Issues," *State Energy Policy: Current Issues, Future Directions,* ed. by Stephen W. Sawyer and John Armstrong. Westview Special Studies in Natural Resources and Energy Management, Boulder, CO. pp. 171–192.

Schiffman, Yale M. and Gregory D'Alessio. 1983. *Limits to Solar and Biomass Energy Growth.* Lexington Books, Lexington, MA.

Schipper, Lee. 1991. "Improved Energy Efficiency in the Industrialized Countries: Past Achievements, CO_2 Emission Prospects." *Energy Policy*, Vol. 19, No. 6.: pp. 127–137.

Shugar, Daniel S. 1991. "Photovoltaics in the Utility Distribution System: The Evaluation of System and Distributed Benefits." Pacific Gas and Electric Company: Research Department, San Ramon.

Shugar, Daniel S., Howard J. Wenger, and Greg J. Ball. 1993. "Photovoltaic Grid Support: A New Screening Methodology." *Solar Today*, Volume 7, Number 5.

Sim, S.S., and S. S. Waters. 1992. *The Competitiveness of Photovoltaics in Electric Utility Supply Side Planning.* Presented at Solar '92 Conference, American Solar Energy Society.

Sioshansi, Fereidoon P. 1991. "The Myths and Facts of Energy Efficiency." *Energy Policy*, Volume 19, No. 3. April.

Sissine, Fred J. 1992. "Renewable Energy: A New National Committment?" Congressional Research Service, Washington, DC.

___. 1990. "Renewable Energy: Federal Programs." CRS Issue Brief, Congressional Research Service, Washington, DC. April.

Sklar, Scott. 1990. "The Role of the Federal Government in the Commercialization of Renewable Energy Technologies," *Annual Review of Energy*. Palo Alto, CA.

Smil, Vaclav. 1991. *General Energetics: Energy in the Biosphere and Civilization*. John Wiley and Sons, New York.

Smutney-Jones, Jan. 1992. "The Eleventh Year of the SO_4 Contracts." Windpower '92. Seattle, WA.

Solar Energy Industries Association. 1993. *Solar Industry Journal*. Vol. 3, Issue 1: pp. 21–32. First Quarter.

____. 1992. *Solar Industry Journal*. Vol. 4, Issue 1: pp. 16–22. First Quarter.

____. 1991. *Solar Industry Journal*. Vol. 2, Issue 1: p. 22. First Quarter.

Solar Energy Research Institute. 1991. *Photovoltaics: New Opportunities for Utilities*. Solar Energy Research Institute, Golden, CO.

____. 1990. *The Potential of Renewable Energy: An Interlaboratory White Paper*. SERI/TP-260-3674. U.S. Department of Commerce, National Technical Information Service, Washington, DC.

____. 1980. *Making Solar Laws Work: A Study of State Solar Energy Incentives*, SERI/TR-722–583.

The Solar Letter. 1993. Volume 3, Number 7.

Spewak, Peter C. 1988. "Analyzing the Effect of Economic Policy on Solar Markets," in R.E. West and F. Kreith, eds., *Economic Analysis of Solar Thermal Energy Systems*. MIT Press: London, England.

Stein, Jay. 1992. "A Study to Determine the Cost-Effectiveness of Active Solar Water Heating as a Demand-Side Management Measure." Boulder, CO. American Solar Energy Society Annual Conference, June 13–18. Cocoa Beach, FL.

Stuntz, Linda. 1991. Internal Memorandum to The Secretary of Energy Re: Spring Planning Process. Department of Energy, Washington, DC.

Sunworld. 1992. International Solar Energy Society. Volume 16, No. 1, p. 23.

Swezey, B and D. Sinclair. 1992. *Status Report on Renewable Energy in the States*. National Renewable Energy Laboratory, Golden, CO.

Swezey, Blair G. and Kevin L. Porter. 1990. "REPiS: The Renewable Electric Project Information System." Solar Energy Research Institute, Golden, CO.

193

Talbot, Allan R. 1983. *Settling Things: Six Case Studies in Environmental Mediation*. The Conservation Foundation and the Ford Foundation, Washington, DC.

Tempchin, Rick. 1993. Unpublished data. Edison Electric Institute, Washington, DC.

Thayer, R.L. and Hansen. 1991. "Wind Farm Siting Conflicts in California: Implications for Energy Policy." University of California, Davis, CA.

Thompson, Wendell. U.S. Energy Information Administration. Washington, DC. Personal communication, 1993.

Tietenberg, Tom. 1988. *Environmental and Natural Resource Economics*. Scott, Foresman and Company, Glenview, IL.

Tolley, George S., Gideon Fishelson, and S. Tiwari. 1989. "A Framework for the Appraisal of Energy R&D." *Resources and Energy*. North Holland.

Toman, Michael. 1991. *The Economics of Energy Security: Theory, Evidence, Policy*. Resources for the Future: Washington, DC.

Totten, Michael and Nita Settina. 1993. *Energywise Options for State and Local Governments*. Center for Policy Alternatives, Washington, DC.

Trexler, Mark. 1991. *Minding the Carbon Store: Weighing U.S. Forestry Strategies to Slow Global Warming*. World Resources Institute, Washington, DC.

Tucker, Mary and Les Tumidaj. 1991. "Solar Access Program for a Large Urban Area." *Proceedings from Solar World Congress*, Vol. 1, Part 11: Pergamon, Oxford.

U.S. Department of Commerce. 1992. *Statistical Abstract of the United States, 112th Edition*. Washington, DC.

U.S. Department of Energy (U.S. DOE). *Five Year Research Plan, 1987–1991*, National Photovoltaics Program, Washington, DC. p. 5.

___. 1991a. *National Energy Strategy: Analysis of Options to Increase Exports of U.S. Energy Technology*. Washington, DC.

___. 1991b. *Natural Gas Monthly*. Washington, DC.

___. 1991c. Unpublished.

___. 1990. *Petroleum Supply Annual*. Washington, DC.

U.S. Department of Energy, Office of Research and Technology Integration. 1989a. *Characterization of U.S. Energy Resources and Reserves*. Washington, DC.

U.S. Department of Energy, Programs in Renewable Energy. 1989b. *Ocean Energy Program Summary: Volume 1: Overview.* Washington, DC.

U.S. Export Council for Renewable Energy. 1992. *Financing Renewable Technologies.* Washington, DC.

U.S. General Accounting Office. 1993. *Electricity Supply: Efforts Under Way to Develop Solar and Wind Energy."* Washington, DC. April.

___. 1987. *Energy R&D, Changes in Federal Funding Criteria and Industry Response.* Report to the Chairman, Subcommittee on Fossil and Synthetic Fuels, Committee on Energy and Commerce, House of Representatives. Washington, DC. February.

___. 1986. *Energy Conservation: Federal Home Energy Audit Program Has Not Achieved Expectations.* Washington, DC. December.

___. 1983. *The Business Energy Investment Credit for Solar and Wind Energy.* Report of the Comptroller General of the United States. Washington, DC. March.

___. 1981. "DOE Needs to Reestablish a Solar Energy Goal and Develop Plans to Achieve That Goal (EMD-81-100)." Letter to Secretary of Energy Edwards from J. Dexter Peach. June 25.

Utility Photovoltaic Group. 1992. *Program Development Plan.* Washington, DC. August.

Varanini, Emilio E. III. 1992. "The Past and Future of Renewable Energy in California." Sacramento, CA.

Vine, E. and J. Harris. 1988. *Planning for an Energy-Efficient Future: The Experience with Implementing Energy Conservation Programs for New Residential and Commercial Buildings, Volume I.* Lawrence Berkeley Laboratory, Berkeley, CA. September.

Vine, Edward and Drury Crawley. 1991. *State of the Art of Energy Efficiency: Future Directions.* American Council for an Energy-Efficient Economy, Washington, DC.

Viscusi, Kip W. and Wesley A. Magat, Mark Dreyfus, William Gentry, and Alan Carlin. 1993. "Interim Draft Report on Efficient Energy Pricing, Project on Economics Research for Long-Term Environmental Risks and Pollution Prevention, Cooperative Agreement with Duke University CA-814388-02." Department of Economics, Duke University, Durham, NC.

Vories, Rebecca and Paul Notari. 1991. "Identifying the Information Needs of Renewable Energy Professionals: An Evaluation of SERI's Technology Transfer Publications." In *Solar World Congress, Vol. 3, Part II*, pp. 3675–3680. Oxford: Pergamon Press. August.

Weinberg, Carl J. and Robert H. Williams. 1990. "Energy from the Sun," *Scientific American*, Volume 263, No. 3, pp. 146–155.

Weissman, Jane. 1993. "PV for Utilities: A National Photovoltaic Strategy for Utilities." December, 1992 workshop at Indian River Conference Center, Stuart, FL.

___. 1992. *PV for Utilities: Developing a National Photovoltaic Strategy for Utilities*. Tuscon, AZ.

West, Ronald E. and Frank Kreith. *Economic Analysis of Solar Thermal Energy Systems*. The MIT Press, Cambridge, MA.

Williams, Susan. 1989. *Power Plays: Profiles of America's Independent Renewable Electricity Developers*. Investor Reponsibility Research Center, Washington, DC.

Wind Energy Weekly. 1992. American Wind Energy Association. Volume 11, Number 488.

Winter, Carl-Jochen. 1991. *To What Extent Can Renewable Energy (RE) Systems Replace Carbon-Based Fuels in the Next 15, 50 and 100 Years?* DLR, Energetics Research Division, Stuttgart, Germany.

Winter, C.-J., W. Meinecke, and A. Neumann. 1990. "Solar Thermal Power Plants: No Need for Energy Raw Materials—Only Conversion Technologies Pose Environmental Questions." DLR, Energetics Research Division, Stuttgart, Germany.

Wirtshafter, Robert M. and Eric W. Hildebrandt. 1992. "Energy Performance Based Connection Fees: A Case Study in New York State." *Energy Policy*, Vol. 20, No. 12.: pp. 1161–1173.

Wood, Frances P. and Roger Naill. 1992. "Using Externalities in Utility Planning: What Will It Cost?" *The Electricity Journal*, Vol. 5, No. 7, pp. 35–43.